Praise for *Zealous for Good Works*

Often when one hears of good works, we are asked to think of salvation and being clear good works do not save. Todd Wilson's *Zealous for Good Works* has used the book of Titus to take a biblical tact. Good works are about mission, evangelism, and key characteristics that build credibility to be the city on a hill, to be what God called His community to be in the world. They show what salvation is for and how mission can be fueled by a walk that matches the talk.

DARRELL L. BOCK
Executive Director for Cultural Engagement, Howard G. Hendricks Center for Christian Leadership and Cultural Engagement; Senior Research Professor of New Testament Studies, Dallas Theological Seminary

God's gospel is not only true and good; it is also beautiful. In this vibrant and practical exposition of Paul's letter to Titus, Todd Wilson argues that the gospel is seen to be beautiful through a demonstration of good works by God's people. Godly living is the goal of the gospel, and this is what is needed to close the church's credibility gap and to make the gospel compelling in today's culture. Wilson helps us to see that Paul's instruction to Titus is as missional as it gets. Those who are tired of chasing the latest ministry fads and who want to listen again to God's Word will be encouraged by this book. I was!

BILL KYNES
Pastor, Cornerstone Evangelical Free Church, Annandale, VA

One of the major challenges for Christ followers today is figuring out how to declare "the gospel" in a world that no longer wants to hear what we have to say. The book of Titus reminds us that it's our good works that raise the curiosity of a watching world, which in turn opens the door of their hearts to our message. It's the church's version of "show and tell"! Of course Titus takes his clue from the words of Christ who, while blessing those who were marginalized for His name's sake, reminded us that we are to be lights in our dark world. And, as Christ notes, that light is our good works, which in turn will draw people to glorify God. Thanks Todd for this relevant and practical guide to practicing our faith in ways that are compelling to a world that, while not listening, is still watching us.

JOE STOWELL
Former President of Moody Bible Institute
President of Cornerstone University

D0206254

As I read Todd Wilson's excellent new book, I was blessed by thinking about many churches that are zealous for good works. But I'm hopeful that through Todd's exposition of Titus, many more Christians will trust in God's grace, which trains us to 'renounce ungodliness and worldly passions, and to live self-controlled, upright, and godly lives in the present age' (Titus 2:12)."

COLLIN HANSEN
Editorial director for The Gospel Coalition and editor of *Our Secular Age: Ten Years of Reading and Applying Charles Taylor*

What a novel idea! A book on how to do mission and ministry based wholly on the Scriptures rather than choosing from among the transient directives of famous ministries. And more, to then ground the ministry on the brief, singular compass of the book of Titus.

But this is where the power of Todd Wilson's *Zealous for Good Works* lies—in the ordered sequence and irrefragable, Spirit-inspired, logic of the apostle Paul's seven practices that will build "a people for his own possession who are zealous for good works" and shine the gospel out to a darkening world.

How grateful I am for the skillful exegesis of Dr. Wilson, a compassionate, seasoned scholar-pastor who lives it out with his wife, Katie, and their children in the bracing climate of Oak Park.

R. KENT HUGHES
Senior Pastor Emeritus of College Church in Wheaton and the John Boyer Professor of Evangelism and Culture at Westminster Seminary in Philadelphia

Zealous for Good Works

MOBILIZING YOUR CHURCH FOR THE GOOD OF YOUR COMMUNITY

Todd A. Wilson

MOODY PUBLISHERS

CHICAGO

Unless otherwise indicated, Scripture quotations are from the ESV® Bible (The Holy Bible, English Standard Version®), copyright © 2001 by Crossway, a publishing ministry of Good News Publishers. Used by permission. All rights reserved.

Scripture quotations marked NIV are taken from the Holy Bible, New International Version®, NIV®. Copyright © 1973, 1978, 1984, 2011 by Biblica, Inc.™ Used by permission of Zondervan. All rights reserved worldwide. www.zondervan.com. The "NIV" and "New International Version" are trademarks registered in the United States Patent and Trademark Office by Biblica, Inc.™

Edited by Kevin P. Emmert
Interior Design: Erik M. Peterson
Cover Design: Dean Renninger
Cover photo of cityscape copyright (c) 2016 by cofotoisme / iStock (623375950). All rights reserved.

Library of Congress Cataloging-in-Publication Data

Names: Wilson, Todd A., 1976- author.
Title: Zealous for good works : mobilizing your church for the good of your
   community / Todd A. Wilson.
Description: Chicago, IL : Moody Publishers, [2018] | Includes
   bibliographical references.
Identifiers: LCCN 2018031607 (print) | LCCN 2018035820 (ebook) | ISBN
   9780802496515 (ebook) | ISBN 9780802416896
Subjects: LCSH: Bible. Titus--Criticism, interpretation, etc. |
   Church--Biblical teaching.
Classification: LCC BS2755.6.C5 (ebook) | LCC BS2755.6.C5 W55 2018 (print) |
   DDC 227/.8506--dc23
LC record available at https://lccn.loc.gov/2018031607

All websites and phone numbers listed herein are accurate at the time of publication but may change in the future or cease to exist. The listing of website references and resources does not imply publisher endorsement of the site's entire contents. Groups and organizations are listed for informational purposes, and listing does not imply publisher endorsement of their activities.

We hope you enjoy this book from Moody Publishers. Our goal is to provide high-quality, thought-provoking books and products that connect truth to your real needs and challenges. For more information on other books and products written and produced from a biblical perspective, go to www.moodypublishers.com or write to:

Moody Publishers
820 N. LaSalle Boulevard
Chicago, IL 60610

1 3 5 7 9 10 8 6 4 2

Printed in the United States of America

To the elders, staff, and
congregation of Calvary Memorial Church.

"For what is our hope or joy or crown of boasting
before our Lord Jesus at his coming? Is it not you?
For you are our glory and joy." (1 Thess. 2:19–20)

Contents

Ancient Wisdom for Today's Church

For over a decade, I had the privilege of serving as the Senior Pastor of Calvary Memorial Church in Oak Park, Illinois. Calvary is a historic church, founded in 1915 as a nondenominational, Bible-teaching church and first pastored by Dr. Louis Talbot, after whom Talbot Theological Seminary was named. The church is located in the heart of Oak Park, one of the country's most politically progressive communities, an urban-suburban village that sits on the border of the city of Chicago.

Oak Park is considered one of the best places in the United States for young professionals to live and is often described as a university town without a university. The village has two patron saints: Frank Lloyd Wright, who had his studio in Oak Park and designed two dozen homes there, and Ernest Hemingway, who was born and reared in Oak Park and graduated from the local high school. Oak Park is a bastion of highly educated liberal elites—a small-scale, more suburban version of Manhattan with a Midwestern twist. Yet the village is surrounded by socioeconomic and cultural diversity with largely Latino communities like Cicero and Berwyn to the south and African American communities like Maywood to the west and Austin to the east.

The church has had a long-standing commitment to the gospel and to this community. As a family of faith, we've longed to be that city on a hill that Jesus talks about in the Sermon on the Mount, one that through our lives radiates the light and life of Christ to others (Matt. 5:14).

But the question has always been *how?* What biblical practices will best empower our church to be a city on a hill in and for Oak Park? How do we as a church let our light so shine before others that they may see our good works and glorify God (see Matt. 5:16)?

The answer for us has come from an unlikely place: the book of Titus. I say unlikely because Titus isn't normally thought of as a go-to for how to think about the ministry and mission of the church. Romans, 1 Corinthians, the Pastoral Epistles, or Acts are all more likely candidates.

But we have found Titus to be a hidden jewel, an oft-overlooked treasure for the church—especially for the church that wants to be a city on a hill whose light shines in the community. I say that for one simple reason: Titus is designed to help followers of Jesus become *zealous for good works*—the kind of good works that are like light that draws others to Christ. As Paul says to Titus, in what is a theologically rich thematic statement at the heart of the book, Jesus Christ has redeemed "a people for his own possession who are zealous for good works" (Titus 2:14).

But this isn't an isolated statement in the short letter. Instead, the whole book is devoted to explaining *how* the grace of God and the gift of Jesus Christ in the gospel does just that—turns sinners saved by grace into believers who are zealous for good works that glorify God and win others to Christ.

In fact, a careful reading of this letter suggests that Paul identifies seven practices, each of which is essential for the church to be what Jesus desires it to be—a city on a hill. Paul begins, naturally enough, with *preaching*, then *leadership*, *teaching, grace, readiness, focus,* and, lastly, *learning.* These are seven practices any church should prioritize and pursue if they want to shine for Christ and make an impact in their community.

This book, then, is an exposition of Titus with particular focus on the theme of mobilizing the church to be zealous for good works, to be a city on a hill. It answers the question many pastors and church leaders are asking: How do I help my church make a difference for Christ? And where can I turn to find sound, biblical advice on how to do this? This book offers time-tested, scripturally based, practical answers that you and your church can put into practice.

While an endless amount has been written on how to help the church become more effective at outreach and evangelism, much of it seems to be a distillation of "best practices" from the nation's largest and most influential churches. The temptation, though, is to look at what's worked at their churches and cut-and-paste it to your own. Sadly, this approach tends to lead to what church consultant Will Mancini has called the "unoriginal sin" of neglecting your church's own uniqueness.[1] Just because a ministry strategy worked at the big megachurch down the road doesn't necessarily mean it's what God wants for your congregation. In fact, I believe that each local church owes it to itself to search the Scriptures afresh and seek the Spirit's leading for its own ministry and mission.

That is what's distinctive about this book. These seven practices aren't the product of extensive field research or interviews with megachurch pastors. Instead, they flow naturally from Scripture itself—indeed, from one book of the Bible, Titus. I'm confident that Titus will speak to many pastors and church leaders who are looking for encouragement and advice but are fatigued with chasing the latest ministry fad and would much prefer to invest their energy into something more solidly rooted in Scripture.

OUR DISCIPLESHIP DEFICIT

I'm excited to explore Titus with you not only because it offers ancient wisdom for the contemporary church, but also because it speaks to some of the leading challenges to the church's witness in the late modern world.

The first challenge is what I call our *discipleship deficit*. It has become cliché to say that North American Christianity is as a mile wide and an inch deep. That is a rather unflattering way of acknowledging that even though forms of evangelical Christianity are widespread in American culture and society, the actual depth and substance of our lives is rather thin. Although we've been good at winning converts, we've not been so good at making disciples. We can fill big churches, but we struggle to grow godly men and women. This is what I mean by our discipleship deficit.

For years, Dallas Willard emphasized this very point. In a 1980 *Christianity Today* article, he wrote,

> For at least several decades the churches of the Western world have not made discipleship a condition of being a Christian. One is not required to be, or to intend to be, a disciple in order to become a Christian, and one may remain a Christian without any signs of progress toward or in discipleship.

He concludes, "So far as the visible Christian institutions of our day are concerned, discipleship is clearly optional."[2]

Why is this? Undoubtedly, a variety of reasons exist: some social, some cultural, some historical. But ultimately, I believe the reason for our discipleship deficit is *theological*: too many preachers and Bible teachers have taught a truncated gospel, one that fails to draw any real link between faith and obedience, or between grace and good works. Again, Dallas Willard identifies the problem: "Obedience and training in obedience form *no intelligible doctrinal or practical unity* with the salvation presented in recent versions of the gospel."[3] The result is that we have people who "believe" the gospel but don't live as Christians, or who "trust" Jesus even though Jesus' will and ways have little to no impact on their lives.

The book of Titus helps redress this discipleship deficit by reminding us that the gospel is fully orbed and that to embrace grace is to experience, inevitably and necessarily, a transformed life—to become a doer of good works. For this is what grace does: it trains us to renounce a life of sin and seek a life of righteousness (Titus 2:11–14).

OUR CREDIBILITY GAP

But there's a second reason why we need to wrestle with the message of Titus. I call it our *credibility gap*. To put it bluntly, evangelicals have a serious "public relations" problem on our hands: those outside the church do not think of us particularly well. David Kinnaman and Gabe Lyons underscored this in their book *unChristian: What a New Generation Really Thinks about Christianity*. We won't rehearse all of their findings here, only to say that, as you are doubtless aware, the word on the street is that evangelicals are, among other things, hypocrites. Kinnaman and Lyons report, "Eighty-five percent of young outsiders have had sufficient exposure to Christians and churches that they conclude present-day Christianity is hypocritical."[4]

It's a stinging accusation, and if we're honest, we have to admit that it sometimes sticks. We don't always live up to our high calling as Christ followers and regularly fall short—and the world takes notice.

Yet I don't think our main problem is *hypocrisy*. Rather, it's *credibility*. My experience leads me to believe that our problem isn't that we say one thing and then knowingly do another. That's hypocrisy. Instead, our problem is that we say one thing and then *unwittingly fail to let that shape the rest of our life*. It becomes an issue of our own trustworthiness. We create a credibility gap between our professed convictions and our actual practice. Put another way, we don't have a heart problem but a circulation problem. It's not that our heart fails to pump blood; it's that the blood doesn't circulate to our daily lives. This lack of circulation—the failure of our convictions to shape our lives—is more of a credibility than a hypocrisy problem. It leaves outsiders to the faith with that niggling question in their mind: "Do those Christians really believe what they're preaching, since it doesn't really seem to shape the practical realities of their daily life? It's as if they're peddling a soda they themselves don't enjoy drinking."

Despite widespread cynicism toward religion in our culture, people are still surprisingly willing to give credit to someone who stands by his convictions—regardless of what those convictions are! In our age of virtual-this and synthetic-that, where everything is accessible but nothing is real, people hunger for something authentic, something credible, something—indeed, *someone*—believable. People long to see someone who lives what he believes.

Here's where the book of Titus comes in. It was written to help the believers on the island of Crete address the issue of credibility in the eyes of outsiders. The argument of the book, in fact, is that we are to devote ourselves to good works for the sake of outsiders, in order to "adorn the doctrine of God our Savior" (2:10). Titus, therefore, calls followers of Jesus to *commend the gospel with credible lives.*

OUR MISSIONAL OPPORTUNITY

There is a third reason why Titus offers a timely message for the twenty-first-century church. It has to do with the church's *missional opportunity.* As you may know, the term *missional* has become a buzzword of late. It's a neologism I personally like, the adjectival form of the noun *mission*, and serves as a catchword for a certain way of both being and living in the world vis-à-vis the non-Christian society around us.

There is, of course, a lot of talk these days about being more "missional." But in my experience, these conversations tend to focus more on form than substance. You're almost left with the impression that being missional has more to do with lighting candles, playing cool music, growing a beard, preaching in jeans, and being a bit edgy than with living a life that is "self-controlled, upright, and godly" (2:12).

I don't want to be unfair, so let me simply ask: When was the last time a "missional" church conference reinforced that the key to missional outreach is the renunciation of sin and the pursuit of holiness or good works? Yet according to Titus, the most effective missional outreach is a congregation devoted to good works. As New Testament scholar Gordon Fee observes, the book of Titus is thoroughly evangelistic in its thrust.[5] Throughout the letter, Paul calls for actions that will be attractive to the world. Good works, then, are for the sake of outsiders.

While we should affirm the need to be more missional and take seriously the widening gap between the church and the post-Christian culture, I'm convinced that the most effective approach to being missional is to cultivate zeal for good works within the life of your local church. When the gospel is seen to be beautiful through a life of good works, then it becomes compelling to outsiders. Being zealous for good works is as missional as it gets.

THE ROAD AHEAD

Let me now sketch for you where we're headed in this book. Chapter 1 sets the context of Titus and introduces you to its message, focusing especially on its emphasis on good works. This chapter expounds three key observations about good works in the book of Titus: good works are everywhere in Titus, good works are essential to authentic faith in Titus, and good works are evangelistic in their thrust in Titus. This sets the stage for the exposition of the seven practices that empower the church to be a city on a hill.

Chapter 2 looks at the opening of Titus (1:1–4) and explores the first of our seven key practices—*preaching*. It is the greatest work in the world, said Martyn Lloyd-Jones. Or as Spurgeon asserted, it can turn a place upside down. It is the most effective way to mobilize the church for outreach to the community. Preaching is unique in its capacity to engage people with the grace of God and stir up in them zeal for good works. This chapter reflects on the origin, content, and purpose of preaching—all with a view to how it serves to turn Christ's followers into a city on a hill.

Chapter 3 focuses on Titus 1:5–16 and addresses a second practice that is vital to effective churches—*leadership*. Good leadership, this chapter argues, begets zeal for good works. And, alternatively, people tend never to rise above their leaders. As go the leaders, so go the people. Which is why leadership, as Titus rightly emphasizes, is so vital to becoming a city on a hill. We will look at Paul's instruction regarding elders—why the church needs elders, what sort of people they should be, and how they can guard the church from nefarious influences that undermine their zeal for good works.

In Chapter 4, we return to the issue of our discipleship deficit as we look at *teaching* as a vital practice for encouraging the community of faith to be a city on a hill. We will look at Titus 2:1–10 and reflect on the kind of teaching ministry Paul envisions for the church—one that emphasizes a correspondence between character and doctrine, leverages relationships to inform hearts and minds, and recognizes that the reputation of the gospel is at stake in all of it.

Chapter 5, "What God Does Matters More," unpacks the fourth key practice—*grace*. Although, because of its content, this chapter could have easily come first. In this chapter, we consider the theological heart of the letter (2:11–14) and reflect on the importance of grace in mobilizing churches to engage in effective outreach. We explore what grace is and what it does, how it stirs us up with zeal for good works. This chapter also includes reflections on how churches can "train" themselves in grace with practices like self-denial and expectant waiting.

Chapter 6 explores the importance of *readiness* if a church is going to be a city on a hill. This chapter shows that followers of Jesus who aspire to be a city on a hill must be prepared to perform their civic and social responsibilities (3:1–2), jettison disdainful attitudes that hinder readiness (3:3), and receive God's gracious salvation continually (3:4–7). "Stop, Look, and Listen," the title to this chapter, is pastor Tim Keller's advice to churches who want to engage more effectively in their communities—and it neatly summarizes the practice of *readiness*.

Chapter 7 draws on something the famous eighteenth-century preacher Charles Spurgeon once said. He liked to talk about John Ploughman, an ordinary guy with extraordinary insights into the Christian life and the ministry of the church. One of his more memorable bits of advice was this: "never stop a plough to catch a mouse." It's a quaint but memorable way of talking about avoiding distractions and staying focused. And it's what Paul encourages the church to be about in Titus 3:8–11—*focus*, another key practice. Chapter 7 discusses how to stay focused and, equally important, what to do with distracting influences in the life of the church.

Chapter 8 looks at the final portion of Titus (3:12–14), which contains the seventh practice—*learning*. Paul encourages Titus, "And let our people learn to devote themselves to good works" (v. 14). This chapter explores how the church becomes zealous for good works by *learning*. This is a learning that comes not by pontificating but by doing, by devoting ourselves to the very thing we want to become more evident in our lives. We will also look at how good works connect to urgent needs, and will consider some powerful and inspiring examples of Christians and churches that are making a profound difference for Christ.

In the final chapter, we will connect these seven practices to Jesus' vision of a city on a hill. To be a city on a hill is Jesus' vision for His people—and it's the aspiration of every pastor I know. The challenge, though, is knowing *how* to help people pursue and embody this vision. We will consider what it means to be a city on a hill, whether your church is a city on a hill, and whether being a city on a hill is a privilege we enjoy or a decision we make.

So join me on this exciting journey together!

CHAPTER 1

Why Titus?

In these pages, you will find seven practices that can help your church be zealous for good works and thus be that city on a hill Jesus talks about in His Sermon on the Mount. We've seen the fruitfulness of each of these practices at work in the life of our local congregation. But I didn't discover these practices through extensive field research; I didn't glean them from interviews with megachurch pastors; and I didn't find them by visiting some of America's fastest growing congregations. Instead, I discovered all seven of them in an unlikely place, the Bible. In fact, in one book of the Bible—Titus.

You may be wondering, *Why Titus?* Surely there are other books of the Bible that are more relevant to the ministry of the church, like Acts or the Pastoral Epistles. Titus doesn't share the same passion and intensity as, say, Galatians, or the same drama and intrigue as 1 or 2 Corinthians. Nor does it contain the same lofty theological peaks as Romans, or the same awe-inspiring imagery as the Revelation. Why Titus, then?

The reason is simple: Titus is designed to help the church become zealous for good works. And zeal for good works is what Jesus envisions for His followers if they're going to be that city on a hill. Jesus says to His followers,

> "You are the light of the world. A city set on a hill cannot be hidden. Nor do people light a lamp and put it under a basket, but on a stand, and it gives light to all in the house. In the same way, let your light shine before others, so that they may see your good works and give glory to your Father who is in heaven." (Matt. 5:14–16)

This is what Jesus envisions for His people. And this, I'm sure, is the aspiration of every person reading this book— that your church would embrace and embody this high calling, to let the light of our lives, as individuals and as communities, shine before others that they may see our good deeds and glorify God.

That's our responsibility as a church. But how do we, practically speaking, live out that calling? How do we faithfully fulfill our responsibility to let the light of our lives shine before others?

Here is where the book of Titus comes in. If we want to be who God is calling us to be, we need to hear and heed the message of the book of Titus.

But what is the message of Titus? The answer may surprise you: zeal for good works. In fact, I think we get to the heart of this book with three simple observations about good works in Titus, three observations that will help you understand this book and help your church take the next step toward being a city on a hill.

GOOD WORKS ARE *EVERYWHERE* IN TITUS

The first observation has to do with the presence of good works in Titus—namely, that good works are *everywhere* in Titus. Read through the letter, and you'll notice that "good works" serves as a steady refrain. In 1:8, for instance, we read that an elder is to be "a lover of good." In 1:16, false teachers are said to "profess to know God, but they deny him by their works. They are detestable, disobedient, unfit for any good work." In 2:7, Titus is charged to show himself "in all respects to be a model of good works." In 2:14, Jesus is said to have purified us that we might be "zealous for good works." And in chapter 3, Christians are called "to be ready for every good work" (v. 1), to be "careful to devote themselves to good works" (v. 8), and to "learn to devote themselves to good works" (v. 14). And these are only the references that *explicitly* mention good works.

Good works also appear in the two key passages of the letter, 2:11–14 and 3:3–8, which are widely recognized to be central to the theological concerns of the letter. Interestingly, in both passages, good works provide the punch line:

> For the grace of God has appeared, bringing salvation for all people, training us to renounce ungodliness and worldly passions, and to live self-controlled, upright, and godly lives in the present age, waiting for

our blessed hope, the appearing of the glory of our great God and Savior Jesus Christ, who gave himself for us to redeem us from all lawlessness and to purify for himself a people for his own possession who are zealous for *good works*. (2:11–14, emphasis added)

But when the goodness and loving-kindness of God our Savior appeared, he saved us, not because of works done by us in righteousness, but according to his own mercy, by the washing of regeneration and renewal of the Holy Spirit, whom he poured out on us richly through Jesus Christ our Savior, so that being justified by his grace we might become heirs according to the hope of eternal life. The saying is trustworthy, and I want you to insist on these things, so that those who have believed in God may be careful to devote themselves to *good works*. (3:4–7, emphasis added)

At the heart of the book of Titus are two passages that center on good works.

Good works also show up in the beginning and end of the letter. The beginning and end of any piece of communication often reveal the intention of that communication, whether it's an email, an eighth-grade term paper, or a New Testament epistle. Notice the closing charge of the book of Titus, the next-to-the-last verse: "And let our people learn to devote themselves to *good works*, so as to help cases of urgent need, and not be unfruitful" (3:14, emphasis added).

And take a look at the opening verse of the letter, which serves as a thematic statement for the whole. There we find an implicit reference to good works: "Paul, a servant of God and an apostle of Jesus Christ, for the sake of the faith of God's elect and their knowledge of the truth, which accords with *godliness*" (1:1, emphasis added). Here, "godliness" means a life of good works, as Paul will go on to explain throughout the rest of the letter.

So you can see that in entitling this exposition of Titus *Zealous for Good Works*, we are getting at the very heart of the message of this letter. Call it the theme or melodic line of the book, if you like. Either way, good works are central to the concern of this New Testament letter. Good works are everywhere in Titus.

GOOD WORKS ARE *ESSENTIAL*
TO AUTHENTIC FAITH IN TITUS

However, as we probe a little further into the book of Titus, we see that it doesn't simply mention good works but also makes an important claim about good works. Specifically, the book of Titus insists that good works are *essential* to authentic faith. In other words, if there is faith, there must be good works. To grasp the truth of the gospel means to live a life of obedience. Good works must always accompany true faith.

Look again with me at the opening verse of the letter: "Paul, a servant of God and an apostle of Jesus Christ, for the sake of the faith of God's elect and their knowledge of the truth, which accords with godliness." That is the ESV rendering of the verse. The NIV interprets the expression so as to draw out the point more explicitly: "Paul, a servant of God and an apostle of Jesus Christ to further the faith of God's elect and the knowledge of the truth *that leads to godliness*" (emphasis added). The point is: authentic faith in God and a genuine knowledge of the truth inevitably leads to godliness, or to a life of good works.

Or take another look at 3:8, where Paul says, "This saying is trustworthy, and I want you to insist on these things, so that those who have believed in God may be careful to devote themselves to good works." Titus, Paul is basically saying, you must insist on these things, these gospel verities I've just mentioned in 3:4–7. Why? So that those who have embraced them by faith may be *diligent to devote themselves to good works.*

As a third example of this theme of the necessity of good works in the life of the believer, look at 1:16. There, Paul is warning of false teachers, and so we have a clear negative example or contrast to this point: "They profess to know God, but they deny him by their works." That's a damning statement to make, isn't it? It cuts to the heart of the message of this book: the necessity of good works in the life of the genuine believer.

Where does this insistence upon the necessity of good works in the life of the believer come from? It comes from an understanding of the gospel, and more specifically, from an understanding of the gospel as *the gospel of good works.*

That may sound jarring to you. We don't often use *gospel* and *good works* in the same sentence, much less the same phrase—unless it is by way of contrast so as to say that the gospel is *not about* good works. "It's not about how many good works you've done," you might say to someone. "We're saved by faith, and not by our good works." Perhaps you've spoken that way, or perhaps you've heard someone speak that way. It's a glorious truth, to be sure, one that is stressed emphatically in Scripture!

Yet in safeguarding the *ground* of the gospel, we can inadvertently downplay the *goal* of the gospel. While the ground of the gospel is grace, the goal of the gospel is good works. What God has done in Christ is grace, sheer grace. There is nothing you can do to add to it. It only needs to be received by faith. But the purpose of this grace in our lives is not to leave us as we are, unchanged. No, the gospel has a goal. This the Bible is equally insistent upon. Listen to how Scripture balances this:

> For by grace you have been saved through faith. And this is not your own doing; it is the gift of God, not a result of works, so that no one may boast. For we are his workmanship, *created in Christ Jesus for good works*, which God prepared beforehand, that we should walk in them. (Eph. 2:8–10, emphasis added)

> [God] saved us and called us *to a holy calling*, not because of our works but because of his own purpose and grace, which he gave us in Christ Jesus before the ages began. (2 Tim. 1:9, emphasis added)

> But when the goodness and loving kindness of God our Savior appeared, he saved us, not because of works done by us in righteousness, but according to his own mercy, by the washing of regeneration and renewal of the Holy Spirit, whom he poured out on us richly through Jesus Christ our Savior, so that being justified

by his grace we might become heirs according to the hope of eternal life. The saying is trustworthy, and I want you to insist on these things, so that those who have believed in God *may be careful to devote themselves to good works.* (Titus 3:4–8, emphasis added)

For the grace of God has appeared, bringing salvation for all people, training us to renounce ungodliness and worldly passions, and to live self-controlled, upright, and godly lives in the present age, waiting for our blessed hope, the appearing of the glory of our great God and Savior Jesus Christ, who gave himself for us to redeem us from all lawlessness and to purify for himself a *people for his own possession who are zealous for good works.* (Titus 2:11–14, emphasis added)

Do you see in these passages the twofold and indeed paradoxical relationship of the gospel to good works? On one hand, we are saved not *because of* good works; on the other, we are saved *for* good works. That's the twofold nature of the gospel's relationship to good works. The gospel is the gospel of good works. Good works are not the ground but the goal of the gospel. For the knowledge of the truth of the gospel leads to godliness, and we are God's workmanship created in Christ Jesus for the very purpose of good works. And that is why the book of Titus, as well as the rest of the New Testament, can insist that good works are not optional, but rather essential to authentic faith.

GOOD WORKS ARE *EVANGELISTIC*
IN THEIR THRUST IN TITUS

So good works are everywhere in Titus. Good works are also essential for Titus. But if we stopped here with these two observations, as important as they both are, we would miss the thrust of the book. We need to make a third and final observation, and it concerns the purpose of good works in Titus. *In Titus, good works are for the sake of outsiders; good works are evangelistic in their thrust.* [1]

A number of years ago, I preached through the book of Titus at our church. I was encouraged to see our congregation catch the vision that good works are evangelistic. Shortly after the series concluded, I was approached by several godly women in our congregation who were stirred by the preaching of the Word and wanted to engage our community of Oak Park more intentionally with the gospel. We met to pray about and discuss what that might look like. In due course, we proposed to start an emergency clothes closet for the homeless living in and around our community. We called it The Closet, and it became one of the most fruitful ministries of our church, serving hundreds of clients in need and commending the beauty of the gospel in the process. Meeting practical needs in our community opened the door to countless opportunities to share the love of Christ in both word and deed, whether through a brief conversation, presenting the hope of the gospel, or praying for God's grace and blessing. The members of our faith family were making good on the vision of Titus as they were becoming more and more zealous for good works.

What we experienced at the ground level is a steady theme in Titus. Yet let me demonstrate this from just two places. In chapter 2, we find instruction on the various ways in which different church members ought to carry out a life of good works: older men are to be sober-minded, dignified, self-controlled; older women are to be reverent; younger men are to be self-controlled, and so on. But notice the purpose behind living this way. On the one hand, negatively speaking, a life of good works *does not detract* from the gospel. We see this in verse 5: younger women are to live such exemplary lives that "the word of God may not be reviled." So too, younger men are, as Paul says to the young man Titus in verses 7–8, called to "show [themselves] in all respects to be [models] of good works, and in [their] teaching show integrity, dignity, and sound speech that cannot be condemned, so that an opponent may be put to shame, having nothing evil to say about us."

On the other hand, positively speaking, a life of good works *commends* the gospel. We see this in verse 10, where we read that slaves are called to be "well-pleasing, not argumentative, not pilfering, but showing all good faith, so that in everything they may adorn the doctrine of God our Savior." Just imagine what a difference it would make if Christians lived in such a way that their lives did not detract from the gospel, that their lives did not detract from the gospel but commended it. Surely, we would find the church's "credibility gap" lessen considerably—and the world would take notice.

Paul continues the theme of good works for the sake of outsiders into chapter 3, where, speaking of the church's conduct in its community, he says to Titus, "Remind them to be submissive to rulers and authorities, to be obedient, to be ready for every good work, to speak evil of no one, to avoid quarreling, to be gentle, to show perfect courtesy toward all people" (vv. 1–2).

The lives of Christians, Paul is saying to Titus, must be exemplary within their community. He reiterates this by way of summary just a few verses later: "The saying is trustworthy, and I want you to insist on these things, so that those who have believed in God may be careful to devote themselves to good works" (v. 8). And he adds the important next sentence: "These things [that is, good works] are excellent and *profitable* for people" (emphasis added).

What's Paul saying? That the good works of the church are profitable for people. How? Not only by blessing their lives, but also by beautifying the gospel of God's grace. Thus, good works are excellent, as Paul says, in themselves, but they are also profitable for people's souls, whether their impact is felt immediately or not.

In Titus, good works serve a vital evangelistic purpose. Good works, of all sizes and shapes and varieties, serve to adorn or commend the gospel. The kind of life we live, both as individuals and as a church, either detracts from the gospel or attracts people to it—and what makes the difference is good works. Do we unsay with our lives what we say with our mouths? Or do our lives attract outsiders to the grace of God found in the gospel?

With Titus, we have a timely and practical evangelistic manual for the twenty-first-century church. This New Testament letter is designed specifically to help us organize and educate for more effective gospel outreach. That truth brings us full circle, to our calling as churches to be that city on a hill that Jesus describes, to be a community that lets our light shine before others so they may see our good works and glorify our Father who is in heaven.

CHAPTER 2

What Turns a Place Upside Down?

My wife, Katie, and I lived in Cambridge, England, for three years while I was a doctoral student at the university. Not far from where we lived, just six miles to the north of downtown Cambridge, is the small village of Waterbeach. It's a rather unremarkable place, save for the fact that Waterbeach was where one the world's finest preachers held his first pastorate.

At age sixteen, Charles Haddon Spurgeon would walk from his home in Cambridge to the village of Waterbeach to preach in an old barn filled with local residents who had come to hear this extraordinary "boy preacher." Already at his young age, Spurgeon was an electrifying preacher—not merely because of his rhetorical gifts but also because of his spiritual power. People regularly met Christ through Spurgeon's preaching. Waterbeach was a rough place, but Spurgeon's ministry was transformative. Years later, he reflected on his first pastoral charge and rejoiced at what God did through his ministry, through his preaching:

> Did you ever walk through a village notorious for its drunkenness and profanity? Did you ever see poor wretched beings that once were men, standing, or rather leaning, against the posts of the alehouse, or staggering along the street? Have you ever looked into the houses of the people, and beheld them as dens of iniquity, at which your soul stood aghast? Have you ever seen the poverty, and degradation, and misery of the inhabitants, and sighed over it? "Yes," you say, "we have." But was it ever your privilege to walk through that village again, in after years, when the gospel had been preached there? It has been mine.[1]

He went on to reflect on the impact his ministry had there:

> There went into that village a lad, who had no great scholarship, but who was earnest in seeking the souls of men. He began to preach there, and it pleased God to turn the whole place upside down.[2]

Preaching—it has the power to turn a place upside down! "There is nothing like it," said one of the twentieth century's great preachers, Martyn Lloyd-Jones of Westminster Chapel, London. "It is the greatest work in the world, the most thrilling, the most exciting, the most rewarding, and the most wonderful."[3]

There is nothing like preaching's capacity to touch hearts and transform lives. There is nothing like preaching to mobilize people to be zealous for good works.

Yet preaching has fallen on hard times. People today often prefer other modes of communication. For many, podcasts and blog posts from their favorite Christian thinkers are more palatable. Preaching has become a bit passé. It's too stuffy, didactic, and authoritative, so this dim view of preaching assumes. Sure, in many churches preaching still has a place in the worship service. But it has lost its service-defining centrality and is no longer thought to be unique among God's ways of building His church. Christian statesman John Stott said many years ago, "The contemporary world is decidedly unfriendly towards preaching."[4]

We should pause, however, to consider whether undervaluing preaching is responsible for the marked decline of spiritual vitality and moral seriousness we see in many of today's churches and Christians. Nearly half a century ago, Lloyd-Jones lamented the decline of preaching and it's impact on the church.[5] It's also worth pondering seriously what I take to be a simple lesson of church history: that the revival of God's people always begins with the revival of preaching. Such was the case during the First and Second Great Awakenings in North America.

At the end of the day, there is nothing like preaching to stir up within God's people a real zeal for good works. Which is why Titus, a biblical book designed to help the church become zealous for good works, opens the way it does—with a statement about preaching.

In this chapter, we take up the first practice designed to make us zealous for good works. Perhaps you noticed that the first four verses of Titus (1:1–4) are jammed full of biblical truth and theological substance. But I suspect you may also have noticed that this passage highlights only one churchly activity—preaching. That's intentional.

As we seek to fulfill our calling to be a city on a hill, as we let our light shine before others that they may see our good works and glorify our Father in heaven, as we adorn the doctrine of God with our Jesus-loving lives, as we pray and strategize and pursue all of these things, we must keep preaching central. *For preaching is the primary way in which God creates a people who are zealous for good works.*

Why is that the case? Because of what preaching is and what preaching does. Preaching is unique in three different ways. First, its origin is in the revelation and command of God. Second, its content proclaims the person and work of Christ, the hope of glory. And third, its purpose is to elicit faith and instill knowledge, which as Paul says, "accords with" or leads to "godliness" (1:1).

THE ORIGIN OF PREACHING:
GOD'S REVELATION AND COMMAND (1:1–3)

Preaching has always been central to the Christian faith. From the earliest days of the apostles, Christians have given themselves to preaching. John Broadus, regarded by many as the father of modern biblical preaching, said this about the place of preaching in Christianity:

Preaching is characteristic of Christianity. No other religion has made the regular and frequent assembling of groups of people, to hear religious instruction and exhortation, an integral part of divine worship.[6]

But why has preaching been a hallmark of Christianity? It has to do with the *origin* of preaching. As we learn from Titus 1:1–3, preaching is rooted in *God's revelation*. In fact, as Paul explains, preaching is the very means by which the purposes and promises of God are manifested to the world. God the Father intended from all eternity past to send God the Son into the world, to redeem us from our sins, and to make for Himself a people for His own possession who are zealous for good works (2:14). This astonishing purpose and these magnificent promises aren't publicized on the evening news, and you won't read about them in *Time* or *Newsweek*. Our only access to them is through the revelation of God.

Preaching is also rooted in *God's command*. The apostle Paul did not make preaching his primary occupation because he liked preaching, because he was good at preaching, or because he earned a good living from preaching. Nor did he give himself to preaching because he got an ego boost from speaking before large crowds. Let's not forget that he was pelted with rocks for preaching God's Word (Acts 14:19)!

No, Paul preached because he was commanded to preach. As he says, preaching is that with which "I have been entrusted by the command of God our Savior" (1:3). This is why Paul identifies himself as "a servant of God" (v. 1). He is a man under authority with clear orders from on high.

This is also why he was called to be "an apostle of Jesus Christ" (v. 1). He is a herald, a steward of the mysteries of God. So Paul says to another young minister, Timothy, "For this I was appointed a preacher and an apostle" (1 Tim. 2:7; see also 2 Tim. 1:11). To the church in Rome, he says it is "my ambition to preach the gospel" (Rom. 15:20). And to the saints of Corinth, "Woe to me if I do not preach the gospel!" (1 Cor. 9:16). For Paul, preaching isn't optional. It's necessary.

Anyone who preaches regularly knows that preaching is not for the faint of heart. As my mentor and former pastor R. Kent Hughes likes to say, "Preaching is the most demanding of intellectual and spiritual tasks." Precisely because it is so demanding—especially when done week in and week out, year after year—preachers can easily find themselves teetering on the brink of burnout, from sheer mental and emotional exhaustion. Every preacher has been there, at least once, if not many times. In those moments, preachers are often tempted to throw in the towel. In those very moments, we need to remind ourselves—and be reminded by others—that preaching finds its source not in ourselves but in a sovereign God who *wills* that preaching exists.

Preaching is rooted in the revelation and command of God. Thus, we would be foolish to treat preaching as insignificant or optional for the church. Rather, preaching is critical and essential to the health and vitality of the church, to your life and mine, even to the flourishing and future of our world. As Spurgeon put it, "Life, death, hell, and worlds unknown may hang on the preaching and hearing of a sermon."[7]

We cannot live without preaching!

THE CONTENT OF PREACHING:
GOD'S WORD AND GOD'S SON (1:3)

A one-of-a-kind activity—that's what preaching is. But what also sets preaching apart from every other activity or mode of communication is its *content*. What is the content of preaching that can be called "Christian"? What is it that we preach? As Paul says, we preach God's Word, not our word (1:3).

Because preaching communicates God's Word, preaching must be both *biblical* and *expository*. Preaching must be biblical because the whole point of preaching is to speak God's Word in human words, not human words in human words. But because preaching is to be biblical, it must be expository. This doesn't mean the preacher must march dutifully through every book of the Bible in order, chapter by chapter, verse by verse, word by word, in some tedious and uninspiring way. Rather, the point is that the preacher must seek to make the message of the text the message of the sermon. What the text says, the preacher must say. Too often, preachers get this backwards. They let what they want to say guide their selection and exposition of Scripture rather than let Scripture itself be their guide.

But in preaching God's Word, we don't merely preach the Bible. We preach *the Christ* of the Bible. The content of preaching is not only the Bible but the One who is the sum and substance of it. For what is the Word of God, from Genesis to Revelation, all about anyway?

In Luke 24, we read about two men who met the risen Christ on the road to Emmaus. Luke says this about Jesus' interaction with these two bewildered disciples: "beginning with Moses and all the Prophets, he interpreted to them in all the Scriptures the things concerning himself" (v. 27). Jesus exegeted Scripture in such a way that He was the central character and narrative thread to all of Scripture. He is both the goal and the key to the entire Bible. He is not only the hope but also the fulfillment of the Old Testament. "For," as Paul says, "all the promises of God find their Yes in him" (2 Cor. 1:20).

In preaching God's Word, then, we preach God's Son. In preaching the Bible, we preach the heart of the Bible, Jesus Christ. In exposing Scripture, we expose ourselves to the Lord of Scripture. "Him we proclaim," Paul says to the Colossians (Col. 1:28). Or to the Corinthians, Paul writes: "what we proclaim is not ourselves, but Jesus Christ as Lord, with ourselves as your servants for Jesus' sake" (2 Cor. 4:5). God's Word and God's Son—this is the content of preaching, which is why there's nothing quite like preaching.

THE PURPOSE OF PREACHING: KNOWLEDGE OF THE TRUTH (1:1)

We also need to appreciate the power and uniqueness of preaching because of the biblically defined purpose of preaching. In a most basic sense, preaching is designed *to elicit or bring forth faith.* How does that happen? As Paul famously says in Romans, "Faith comes from hearing, and hearing through the word of Christ" (10:17). Preaching is God's means of making known the Word of Christ so that faith might spring to life in the hearts of God's people— those whom God has chosen to be heirs of salvation.

More precisely, this means that preaching is designed *to instill in God's people a knowledge of the truth*. Notice that when Paul pairs "the faith of God's elect" with "their knowledge of the truth" in 1:1, he further defines the first phrase with the second.[8] Here, faith is equated with knowledge of the truth.

Because preaching instills in us a knowledge of the truth, it cures us of the most fatal of diseases—ignorance.[9] Think about it. How much of our spiritual malaise and immaturity results from not knowing the truth of God's Word? This should be no great surprise to us. As my former pastor Kent Hughes liked to say, "We cannot be profoundly impacted by that which we do not know!"

The sad reality, however, is that many of us know far more about our favorite sports team, our favorite hobby, or our line of work than we do about the Word of God. In fact, there is a startling degree of biblical illiteracy among Bible-believing Christians. And while biblical literacy or knowledge of the truth leads to godliness, biblical illiteracy or biblical ignorance inevitably leads to spiritual impotence and ineffectiveness.

Yet when faith comes to life in one's heart and the knowledge of the truth of God's Word has renewed one's mind, the result is always *a transformed life*. Indeed, the result is a life that is increasingly zealous for good works. For the knowledge of the truth, as Paul says, "accords with" or leads to "godliness" (1:1), to a life of good works.

A number of years ago during the Christmas season, *The Times* published a remarkable article that underscores what we're talking about in this chapter. That this secular news outlet should publish a piece on God was striking enough— and all the more that it was written by a self-proclaimed atheist. The article had the arresting title, "As an atheist, I truly believe Africa needs God."[10]

Its author, Matthew Paris, describes visiting the African country of Malawi and several charity works there. In response to what he saw, he wrote,

> It inspired me, renewing my flagging faith in development charities. But travelling in Malawi refreshed another belief, too: one I've been trying to banish all my life, but an observation I've been unable to avoid since my African childhood. It confounds my ideological beliefs, stubbornly refuses to fit my world view, and has embarrassed my growing belief that there is no God.

He added,

> Now a confirmed atheist, I've become convinced of the enormous contribution that Christian evangelism makes in Africa: sharply distinct from the work of secular NGOs, government projects and international aid efforts. These alone will not do. Education and training alone will not do. In Africa Christianity changes people's hearts. It brings a spiritual transformation. The rebirth is real. The change is good.

Do you see that astonishing confession, from an atheist no less? *Christianity changes people's hearts. It brings spiritual transformation. The rebirth is real. The change is good.* That sounds a lot like Spurgeon's experience when his preaching turned the village of Waterbeach upside down. That sounds a lot like the experience of many preachers and evangelists down through the ages of the church. Perhaps that matches your experience.

The primacy of preaching is changing people's hearts, promoting spiritual transformation, affecting new birth, initiating change, making people zealous for good works!

Whether in Africa or America, Malawi or the Midwest; whether among the poor or the rich, the uneducated or the educated; whether in the first century or the twenty-first century—there is simply nothing like preaching!

PREACH THE WORD

Preaching is the primary way in which God creates a people who are zealous for good works. I have seen this time and again in my own preaching ministry, and I suspect it resonates with your own church experience, too. Whether it's calling our congregation to greater financial generosity or increased evangelistic intentionality, over and over it begins with preaching, relying on the power of God's Word, and Christ's voice to speak to our hearts in a way that catalyzes genuine response.

Of course, preaching isn't the only way that God creates a people who are zealous for good works, as we shall see as we work our way through the book of Titus. But we need to be clear at the outset: preaching is indeed the *primary* way God does so. Of all the practices and qualities that we will explore in this book, preaching is the main one. That's why Paul begins this short letter the way he does.

But if preaching is primary, then our challenge is to order our lives as individuals and churches so that, as they say, we keep the main thing the main thing. If your church is going to be a city on a hill, then it's going to have to insist on the primacy of preaching and allow no substitutes.

This is why Paul was so insistent with his junior colleague in the ministry, Timothy, that he must "preach the word; be ready in season and out of season; reprove, rebuke, and exhort" (2 Tim. 4:2). Paul says the same thing to Titus: "Declare these things; exhort and rebuke with all authority. Let no one disregard you" (2:15). It's as if the veteran pastor and preacher, the apostle Paul, is pleading with his understudies, "Brothers, the main thing is to keep the main thing the main thing!" In other words, "Preach the Word!"

Preaching must be central and shape everything a church does. And let me say, as a preacher, that we must insist on preaching as central not because the *preacher* is central, but because *God* and *His Word* are central.

This is also why congregations must help their pastors prioritize preaching. Pastors aren't only preachers; they have a whole world of other responsibilities. Sadly, these other responsibilities, important though they be, can eat up all of the pastor's time and drain him of all his energy. Pastors need congregants who encourage them not to neglect the main thing—the preaching of God's Word. This may mean sacrifice on the church's part because the pastor may not be able to be as present or available as either he or the church would ideally like. But the sacrifice will be worth it in the long run. The church will flourish as the pulpit does.

Finally, each one of us needs to prioritize the preaching of the Word in our own life. What is the high point of your week? Is it sitting under the ministry of God's Word? If not, why not? For what could be more thrilling than the prospect of hearing the voice of God speaking to you in words you can understand? When you prioritize the preaching of God's Word in your own life, you will come to a greater knowledge of the truth that leads to good works.

CHAPTER 3

You'll Never Rise Above Your Leader

I have a booklet that reviews the first six decades of Calvary Memorial Church's history, from the founding of the church in 1915 to the church's relocation to 931 Lake Street in downtown Oak Park in 1979. The booklet was created for the dedication service of the church's new building. President Jimmy Carter wrote a congratulatory letter that was read to the congregation, and Dr. Billy Graham preached the message. The church had arrived, by the grace of God, at a wonderful place: its people were growing, and its ministries were thriving. The booklet was aptly entitled "A History of Great Decisions." That's what the first six decades represented.

In my view, however, one of the greatest decisions the church ever made came a decade later, when my predecessor, Dr. Ray Pritchard, invited the church to reconsider its polity and leadership structure. At the time, the church had a leadership board comprised of the heads of various committees. Dr. Pritchard advocated that the church move to what he argued was a more biblical model of church governance and leadership: a plurality of elders.

This was one of the great decisions of the church. While it's true that preaching is the primary way in which God stirs up zeal for good works in His people, the next most important thing for a church in this regard is *leadership*.

Leadership is so powerful that churches are either killed by bad leadership or thrive on good and godly leadership. It's a truism in life and in the life of the church: as goes the leadership, so goes the church. In fact, a church never rises above the spirituality of its leaders. That's why leadership is vital.

The main point of this chapter is that *good leadership begets zeal for good works*. Conversely, bad leadership undermines zeal for good works. That is the gist of Titus 1:5–16, a passage about elders and the critical role they play within the life of the church.

Most readers of this book will have at least heard of elders. Perhaps you serve at a church that has elders. But you may not be entirely sure who they are or what they do. You know what the pastor does—or is supposed to do. But the elders? That's far less obvious. What is more, you're not sure why the church has them—much less why the church absolutely needs them.

In his book *Biblical Eldership*, Alexander Strauch describes arriving at a concert being held at a church, and there in the foyer finding prominently displayed the picture of the senior pastor and underneath it, in the form of a pyramid, the rest of the pastoral staff. Then, as he went down the hallway toward the washroom, out of sight and mind, he came across a glass case with pictures of the elders.[1]

What a perfect illustration of how elders are often viewed within the life of a church! Even in churches with elders, they're often an inconspicuous group of folks. You hardly ever see them or hear from them—except when there is some exceptionally bad news the paid staff would rather not share. Then, and only then, you get a letter from "The Elders."

This, of course, is understandable, because we have on the whole failed to teach on the role of elders within the church. Our passage in Titus should correct the deficiency. What we find in this passage is a simple yet powerful argument about how the church ought to organize itself for effective gospel outreach. And the argument is all about elders.

The passage unfolds in a series of steps. First, the church needs elders (v. 5). Second, the church needs elders with character and conviction (vv. 6–9). And third, the church needs godly elders to protect the church from ungodly influences (vv. 10–16).

THE CHURCH NEEDS ELDERS (1:5)

This passage argues first that *the church needs elders*. We learn this from the first verse, which introduces us to the body of the letter and provides important information about the purpose of Titus and the circumstances in which it was written.

Like Timothy, Titus was one of Paul's most loyal and trusted junior colleagues in ministry. Titus plays prominently in Paul's ministry in Corinth, as we learn from Paul's second letter to the church in that city (2 Cor. 2:13; 7:6,

13–14; 8:6, 16, 23; 12:18; cf. Gal. 2:1–3; 2 Tim. 4:10). Upon release from house arrest in Rome, Paul made his way back to Ephesus by way of the Mediterranean island of Crete. And there, as he says in this opening verse, he left Titus.

But Paul didn't ditch Titus in Crete. He strategically deployed him for gospel purposes. Titus had an important commission on the island of Crete. Paul reminds him, "This is why I left you in Crete, so that you might put what remained into order, and appoint elders in every town as I directed you" (Titus 1:5). Titus was to put what remained into order. In doing so, he was to appoint good and godly leaders (that is, elders) in every town on that island. And notice that Paul has already given Titus this directive ("as I directed you").

This letter is a follow-up intended to provide Titus with the encouragement and authority he needs to get on with it—*to organize the church for effective gospel outreach by appointing good and godly leaders or elders.*

We learn from this opening verse, then, that Paul believed appointing elders was critical for the churches in Crete. We'll explore why as we move through the passage. But for now, note that this directive to appoint elders is not unique to the book of Titus. Nor was the appointment of elders unique to the churches in Crete.

Evidently, this was Paul's common practice. Wherever he planted churches, there he appointed elders. We read in Acts of Paul and Barnabas: "And when they had appointed elders for them in every church, with prayer and fasting they committed them to the Lord in whom they had believed" (14:23; see also Phil. 1:1).

Yet appointing elders was not unique to Paul. In fact, what we find in the New Testament is that *eldership is the consistent pattern of leadership for the local church,* whether it be the church in Jerusalem (Acts 15:2), the church in Ephesus (Acts 20:17), or the churches in Pontus, Galatia, Cappadocia, Asia, and Bithynia (1 Peter 1:1; 5:1).

The common thread in all these churches is a plurality of elders. Elder leadership, then, appears to be one of the only organizational expectations we can glean from the New Testament. The Bible doesn't have a lot of specific guidance on church polity or governance structures, but it is consistent in its insistence on elder leadership.

We are wise to remember that much of what we do as a church—how we organize ourselves and how we design our ministries—is not biblically required. That is, the New Testament doesn't provide clear directives or instruction on much of what we do. This doesn't call into question what we do as an organization or make it suspect. It simply means that some of our organizational structures and leadership decisions are optional, not essential.

Biblically speaking, do we need a Nominating Committee? No. Do we need a Pulpit Committee? No. Do we need to have two congregational meetings a year? No. And at those congregational meetings, do we need to observe the latest version of *Robert's Rules of Order*? No. Do we need ushers or greeters or a hospitality team or a choir or custodians or even a building? No, we don't. Of course, we're grateful for each of these, as they've served the church well and effectively. But we won't be out of step with the New Testament without any of them.

We will be out of step with Scripture, however, if we fail to have elders. *The church needs elders.* Because, as we see from Titus, elders help churches become and be zealous for good works.

THE CHURCH NEEDS ELDERS
WITH CHARACTER AND CONVICTION (1:6–9)

But what kind of elders does the church need? Does the church need elders with a particular education or training or credentials? Does an elder need business experience? Does he need to be well connected, a power broker within the church? Does he need to be wealthy? Does he always need to see eye-to-eye with the pastor?

Of course, these and many similar characteristics are thought to be important to the role and work of an elder. But these are pseudo-qualifications that have no support in Scripture. Titus 1:6–9 reminds us there are two critical qualifications for an elder: character and conviction. An elder must be a man of irreproachable character, and he must be a man of deep biblical conviction. Hence, the second step in the argument of this passage: *the church needs elders with character and conviction.*

First, an elder must be a man of *irreproachable character.* Paul makes this point in verses 6–8, where twice he says that an elder must be "above reproach" (vv. 6–7). This means he must be free from accusation—literally, not able to be reproached, whether from those within or outside the church.

Conversely, he must enjoy a good reputation among Christians and non-Christians alike. Being an elder, like being a pastor, is a public role. It's necessary, then, that not only the church, but also the community, be able to speak well of the character of the leadership of the church. Think about it: How might your church's effort to advance the gospel in your community suffer if you were to put in a leadership position someone with a poor reputation in your community? This is why it is good that the congregation is involved in the selection process so that they can help corroborate publicly the good reputation of any elder that would serve in leadership.

From this passage, we learn an elder must be above reproach in two respects. First, he must be above reproach *in his home life*: "the husband of one wife," Paul insists, "and his children are believers and not open to the charge of debauchery or insubordination" (v. 6). Both of these statements have generated quite a bit of discussion and debate over the years, largely because we slip into thinking that Paul is trying to make some overly technical point.[2] What he's insisting on is simply that *if* a man is married and *if* he has children, then he must be a faithful husband and a faithful father—that is, he must be faithful at home. Otherwise, we have no reason to believe that he will be faithful in the church.

So if you aspire to lead in the church, then don't neglect your home. For when it comes to leadership, the home is the training ground for the church. Or as someone has astutely observed, "A good look at the man's home life will tell much about his character and his ability to give leadership to the church."[3]

There's a second respect in which an elder must be above reproach: *in his overall pattern of life*. We see this emphasis in verses 7b–8, where Paul provides a general list of five vices and six virtues that together paint a picture of the kind of character that is required of one who would serve in church leadership: "He must not be arrogant or quick-tempered or a drunkard or violent or greedy for gain, but hospitable, a lover of good, self-controlled, upright, holy, and disciplined."

Interestingly, note that there is nothing here that is not expected of *every* Christian. If you're not an elder, that doesn't mean you can be arrogant or hot-headed or drink too much wine. Similarly, every Christian—whether or not they serve in leadership—ought to be hospitable, a lover of good, self-controlled, upright, holy, and disciplined. These aren't qualities just for elders, but for every Christian. The only difference is that these are *qualifications* for those who would serve as elders. They aren't ideals but prerequisites.

But why, you may be wondering, *is character so critical to leadership?* It is, after all, incredibly countercultural in modern society for the Christian church to insist on certain moral prerequisites before serving in leadership. You won't find anything like this if you serve in leadership in the Rotary Club or the School Board or the Peace Corps—nor, sadly, if you run for congress, the senate, or president!

The reason it's so critical that an elder be a man of irreproachable character is because of who an elder is in God's sight. As the beginning of verse 7 tells us, "An overseer, *as God's steward*, must be above reproach" (emphasis added). Elders must be good and godly because they are God's stewards and oversee His house, the church. An elder is a father to a local church family; he oversees and cares for the family of faith. And as we're all very well aware, a good and godly father is a force of great good within a home, whereas a bad and self-serving father is a force of great harm within a home. So, too, elders in the church.

An elder should also be a man of *biblical conviction*. Paul makes this point in verse 9: "He must hold firm to the trustworthy word as taught, so that he may be able to give instruction in sound doctrine and also to rebuke those who contradict it."

Elders must first know what Paul refers to here as "the trustworthy word as taught"—that is, they must know the gospel and the contours of biblical revelation. Elders must be men of the Book. They should know their Bibles and know them well.

But simply knowing the Word is not enough for an elder to be well qualified. They must *hold firmly* to the Word as well. They need to have a tenacious grip on biblical truth. So, for example, when it comes to talking about the basic story line of the Bible or the great doctrinal truths of the Christian faith, elders must be able to speak with confidence and conviction. You need to sense that they've got their head around this Book—and that this Book is penetrating their heart.

The reason elders need to have a firm grasp on God's Word is because they have a vital, twofold teaching task within the life of the church: they must be men of solid biblical conviction so that, as Paul says, they can "give instruction in sound doctrine," on the one hand, and "rebuke those who contradict it," on the other (v. 9). They need to be ready and willing to go the distance in fidelity to God's Word.

The great Protestant pastor and theologian John Calvin

talked about the need for elders and pastors to have two voices: one to gather the sheep and feed the flock with biblical instruction, and the other to drive away the wolves with words of sharp rebuke and warning.[4]

Regrettably, I suspect that in too many churches today, only one of these two voices is ever heard: the voice of instruction feeding the sheep. That, of course, is a vitally important voice. But it's not the only voice that needs to be heard. When it is the only one, and the sheep have no corresponding voice of rebuke to drive away the wolves, then the sheep are left exposed, vulnerable to the attack of wolves. "Beware," Jesus warned, "of false prophets, who come to you in sheep's clothing but inwardly are ravenous wolves" (Matt. 7:15).

GODLY ELDERS PROTECT THE CHURCH
FROM UNGODLY INFLUENCES (1:10–16)

This stark warning of Jesus leads us on to the third step in the argument of this passage: *the church needs godly elders to protect the church from ungodly influences.*

According to the New Testament, an elder has several different responsibilities. First, elders are to *lead* by governing and directing the affairs of the church. Second, elders are to *feed* the church by teaching the Word of God. Third, elders are to *care* for the spiritual needs of the church by praying for the sick, for example, and anointing them with oil (James 5:14). And fourth, elders are to *shepherd* the church by protecting the flock from harm.[5]

Because of the situation in the churches on the island of Crete, Paul felt compelled to elaborate on this fourth responsibility in his letter to Titus. It's critical that Titus appoint elders in every town (v. 5), elders with both character and conviction (vv. 6–9), because, as Paul goes on to explain, there are many who if left to themselves would surely undermine the health and vitality of the church (vv. 10–16). As Paul explains, "There are many who are insubordinate, empty talkers and deceivers" (v. 10a).

Now, in case it's not obvious, let me say that people who are insubordinate and who use deception as tools of influence within the life of the church—they kill churches. That's been my experience, and it may be your experience. It certainly was Paul's experience. The false teachers on the island of Crete were evidently creating quite an uproar. They were, as Paul says in verse 11, "upsetting *whole families* by teaching for shameful gain what they ought not to teach" (emphasis added).

Why is it that false teachers can have such a negative impact upon the church? The main reason is they dupe the unsuspecting with their profession of faith. That is, they sound like Christians and may even, at least from a distance, look like Christians. And so they pull the proverbial wool over many eyes and thus are able to masquerade within the church as wolves in sheep's clothing.

Further, because they love neither God nor the Son of God, they focus instead on what is important *to them*—not the gospel, but what is tangential or peripheral to the gospel. This is precisely what was going on in Crete. The false teachers were majoring on what was tertiary at best, "devoting themselves to Jewish myths and the commands of people who turn away from the truth" (v. 14).

So even though they "profess to know God," it is nothing less than a sham. There is nothing redemptive in their heart and so nothing transformative in their life. While they talk big about God and the gospel, they "deny him by their works" (v. 16a). The bottom line is this: false teachers are morally unfit to lead others to good works. "They are detestable," as Paul says, "disobedient, unfit for any good work" (v. 16b).

Notice, then, how this reality connects to godly elders and ungodly influences: godly elders are critical to the vitality of the church because they can deal with the ungodly influences that undermine the church's zeal for good works. Godly leadership begets good works in the life of a church. Ungodly leadership undermines good works in the life of a church.

That is why Paul doesn't beat around the bush when discussing how to handle ungodly influences within the church. "They must be silenced," he insists to Titus in verse 11. How? By offering them a sharp rebuke, as he has said in verse 9 and now in verse 13: "rebuke them sharply." The goal is not to humiliate but to heal—that they would be silenced, yes, but ultimately that they would be "sound in the faith" (v. 13).

Regrettably, however, a sharp rebuke offered in love by elders doesn't always work, which is perhaps why at the end of the letter Paul circles back to this issue of how to handle ungodly influences within the church. In 3:10–11, he instructs his junior colleague in the ministry, "As for a person who stirs up division, after warning him once and then twice, have nothing more to do with him, knowing that such a person is warped and sinful; he is self-condemned."

Rebuke, rebuke, then disregard. This is the pattern for how to deal with insubordinate, empty talkers and deceivers who would seek to take advantage of the unsuspecting within the church. Needless to say, this is difficult work that requires both fortitude and humility. That's why the role of an elder is not for the faint of heart or the weak-kneed. But it's also not for the arrogant or quick-tempered (Gal. 6:1). Instead, the church needs men of character and conviction and, we might now add, courage.

CONCLUSION

It was one of Calvary Memorial's greatest decisions to move toward a more biblical form of church leadership—to a plurality of elders. The congregation has been the beneficiary of untold blessings because of this Spirit-led decision many years ago. The elders have been faithful to their biblical calling and have raised the spiritual vitality of the congregation. As the leaders, so the people. Zealous elders, zealous congregation.

One of the most profound ways in which the elders have encouraged the church toward good works has been through their commitment to prayer. Each week the church leadership receives hundreds of prayer requests from the members of the congregation. And each week the elders pray faithfully through these requests. More than that, on a quarterly basis, the elders reach out by phone to each and every one who has submitted a prayer request to check on the status of their request, to encourage them in their walk with Christ, and to pray for them in person. The fruit from this simple practice has been immense—even though we know only the light of eternity will reveal the full impact of their prayer support!

I appreciate the way Calvary's constitution defines the role of an elder. One of the points that it states about elders reads, "Refute Those Who Contradict Truth," and provides the supporting scriptural reference from Titus 1:9. Further,

> Elders are to confront those who teach doctrine contrary to the Articles of Faith or who continue in a pattern of behavior contradictory to Biblical truth. Thus, Elders are to guard against the strategies of Satan, so that the truth of Christ will remain credible to both the congregation and the community.

This is why we need good and godly leaders in the life of this church. This is why we need elders, men of deep personal character and solid biblical conviction. We need elders to guard against the strategies of Satan and to ensure the credibility of the gospel within the church and in the community. We need elders to help us become zealous for good works.

Next to the ministry of preaching, nothing is more critical for the life of the local church than good and godly leadership. Bad leadership kills churches. Good and godly leadership, on the other hand, is a mighty force for good in helping a people become zealous for good works.

CHAPTER 4

Fixing the Discipleship Deficit

To describe American evangelicalism as a mile wide but an inch deep is cliché, no doubt, but it is partially true. While many Americans would profess some kind of evangelical faith, commitment to and knowledge of the faith is alarmingly thin. We're good at winning converts but not so good at making disciples. We can fill large churches, but we struggle to grow mature Christians.

Evangelical Christianity suffers from what I referred to earlier as a *discipleship deficit*. That's a way of describing the struggle we have in teaching people how to live the Christian life. No one in recent years has written as thoughtfully on this problem as Dallas Willard. In fact, he hammered on this theme for years, evidently to little avail. Back in 1980, he wrote in an article for *Christianity Today*:

> For at least several decades the churches of the Western world have not made discipleship a condition of

being a Christian. One is not required to be, or to intend to be, a disciple in order to become a Christian, and one may remain a Christian without any signs of progress toward or in discipleship.[1]

He concludes, "So far as the visible Christian institutions of our day are concerned, discipleship is clearly optional."[2]

How do we address the discipleship deficit that Willard described decades ago and yet remains today? We address it, at least in part, by doing what Paul calls Titus to do in the opening verse of chapter 2 of his letter: "teach what accords with sound doctrine." *Teaching God's Word catalyzes zeal in God's people, helping them become a city on a hill.*

Preaching is primary in God's economy (1:1–4). Leadership is next in line (1:5–16). And when both biblical preaching and godly leadership are in place, the next element the church needs is *teaching* (2:1–10).

The main point of this passage in Titus, and of this chapter, is that the church has a responsibility to teach. This is Paul's main point to Titus in 2:1. Everything else he says in chapter 2 elaborates on that charge. He is advising Titus on both *how* he ought to teach and *what* he ought to teach.

This passage, therefore, helps us think about the teaching ministry in your church: what you ought to focus on and how you ought to go about it. From this passage, we can draw three observations about the teaching ministry of the church. Or consider them three theses about the teaching ministry of your church that will catalyze zeal for good works in your people.

TEACH THE CHARACTER THAT
CORRESPONDS TO THE CHRISTIAN FAITH

Our first thesis is this: *churches should teach the character and conduct that corresponds to Christian faith*. This is the first point in this passage, and this is exactly what Paul calls Titus to do: "But as for you, teach what accords with sound doctrine" (2:1).

If you're reading an ESV Bible—the translation I normally prefer to read—then you may see included what I take to be an unfortunate heading that the editors have given to this passage: "Teach Sound Doctrine." But Paul does not say, "But as for you, teach sound doctrine." Rather, he says, "teach *what accords with* sound doctrine" (emphasis added).

Of course, teaching sound doctrine is implied in this exhortation. And elsewhere in this letter, Paul underscores both the necessity and importance of teaching sound doctrine. As we saw earlier, an elder must "hold firm to the trustworthy word as taught, so that he may be able to give instruction in sound doctrine" (1:9). This means elders and teachers must know the Word of God and the contours of the gospel, and be able to teach them faithfully. They must teach sound doctrine.

But here in this passage, and in this opening verse, Paul calls Titus to teach something else—or, perhaps better, *something more*. Titus must teach not just sound doctrine, but also *what accords with* sound doctrine. What is that? Well, look at what Paul does in the rest of this passage. He himself teaches what accords with sound doctrine. And with a quick glance, we see what he's teaching: godly character and conduct.

So, Titus is to teach the church both sound doctrine and sound *ethics*. He's to instruct the church not only in what Christians are to believe about God and the gospel, but also how they should live in light of who God is and what God has done in and through the gospel. This is what it means to teach *what accords with* sound doctrine. We're to teach the character and conduct that corresponds to Christian faith.

In my experience, churches tend to fall short of the responsibility to teach what accords with sound doctrine in one of two ways. One way is by simply teaching more and more sound doctrine, as though pumping people full of doctrine alone will somehow make them holier. But simply offering another Bible study on Romans won't necessarily help anyone love their spouse or serve their neighbor more faithfully.

The other way we fall short is by assuming that all we need to do is get people to sign off on sound doctrine and all will be well—as though simply professing sound doctrine is the same as living in accordance with sound doctrine. This is where the false teachers in Crete went awry: they divorced doctrine from ethics. They professed to know God but denied Him with a life that did not accord with sound doctrine (1:16). That's why Paul begins this verse the way he does: "But as for you . . ." Titus's teaching is to contrast sharply with that of the other teachers described in 1:10–16.

So what should this teaching that accords with sound doctrine look like? We note two qualities from what Paul says in verses 2–10 of chapter 2. First, it is to be *comprehensive*. This does not mean exhaustive, where you cover absolutely everything. Rather, it means you address that which is of first importance, and you do so as they apply to and are relevant for the diverse types of people in the local church. Notice that Paul offers instruction to people of all ages and of both genders: first, to the older men (v. 2) and then the older women (v. 3); next, to the young women (vv. 4–5) and then young men (vv. 6–8). He also includes a word to slaves (vv. 9–10) because they too were an important part of the ancient household. Thus, he offers instruction to every station in life.

Second, we note that this teaching is to be *concrete*. Sometimes we content ourselves in our teaching vague generalities. Paul doesn't. He speaks concretely about the kind of character and conduct that corresponds to sound doctrine. "Older men," he says very plainly, "are to be sober-minded, dignified, self-controlled, sound in faith, in love, and in steadfastness" (v. 2). "Older women likewise," he continues, "are to be reverent in behavior, not slanderers or slaves to much wine" (v. 3). Young women are to "love their husbands and children, to be self-controlled, pure, working at home, kind, and submissive to their own husbands" (vv. 4–5). Young men are to be, well, what young men often struggle to be: self-controlled (v. 6). And slaves: they're not to be argumentative or to steal, but to be full of integrity and well pleasing to those they serve (vv. 9–10).

This is all very specific and concrete, even in your face at points. We need to teach this way—calling out specific vices to avoid and holding up behaviors we should seek to emulate. This is the kind of teaching that will save the church from nominal Christianity and easy-believism. It's also the kind of teaching that will nourish the more mature members.

Ajith Fernando, the national director of Youth for Christ

in Sri Lanka, writes about the situation of the church in Sri Lanka that drives home this precise point:

> I was once talking to a pastor working in an unreached area of Sri Lanka about the struggle to nurture godly believers among recent converts to Christianity. We talked about how important it is to explain the Christian lifestyle and to address areas of unholiness that we are seeing in the church. He said that most pastors today avoid doing that because it brings up many questions that are difficult to handle. People come to Christ because he meets their needs, not because they want to be holy. If we talk about particular issues of holiness, they are turned off and leave the church. So pastors avoid addressing these issues. If this is allowed to continue, we will soon have a highly nominal church.[3]

The church is responsible, then, to teach character and conduct that corresponds to the Christian faith. And it must be intimately related to our understanding of the gospel and God's grace as it has appeared in Jesus Christ. There can be no divorce of Christian conduct and Christian doctrine.

LEVERAGE OUR RELATIONSHIPS
TO TEACH CHRISTIAN LIVING

While the opening verse of this passage is addressed to Titus, we recognize he's not the only one called upon to teach what accords with sound doctrine. It's not only Titus's job to teach the character and conduct that corresponds to the Christian faith. No, we see in verse 2 that older men are called to exemplify for the entire congregation a way of life that suits their station in life. We see in verses 3–4 that older women are also called to "teach what is good" to the younger women. And we see in verses 6–8 that Titus, a young man himself, is to model for and thus teach other young men what a godly life looks like.

So we see from these verses that the teaching ministry of the church extends well beyond Titus himself. In fact, we realize that the vast majority of the teaching that should happen in the life of the local church happens not in formal ways through one particular pastor or leader but in a thousand informal ways and through various relationships among members in the church. In other words, the whole congregation should be engaged in the teaching ministry. Which brings us to our second thesis: *churches should leverage relationships to teach the character and conduct that corresponds to Christian faith.*

But how? Through two principal means: *modeling* and *mentoring.* Think about it. Who does the majority of the teaching in this church? The pastor or congregants?

While it may sound counterintuitive at first, we have to say that the vast majority of the teaching that touches lives in our churches is done neither by the pastor nor at church on Sunday. The vast majority of the teaching happens off-site—in homes and workplaces, driving to school or to your son's soccer game, sitting around the kitchen table, kneeling by the bed, tucking the kids in at night.

In your church and mine, the vast majority of the teaching that touches lives comes about through the ordinary, everyday interactions of the members of our churches, as they get together over coffee, talk on the phone, meet for a play date, go out for dinner, exchange texts or emails, connect for prayer, and so on.

That is why we must leverage these relationships if we're going to see the church instructed in how to live the Christian life. This is why, for example, we have prioritized geographically based small groups. They've proven to be a remarkably effective way of helping people get into one another's lives on a weekly, if not daily, basis. People connect, thick relationships form, and lives are touched and changed. Every interaction that members of our churches have with other Christians is an opportunity for modeling the Christian life and mentoring another person in the faith.

And what a powerful teacher modeling and mentoring can be! Andrew Murray, a great devotional writer, wrote a powerful book on parenting. At the outset of the book, he makes an important point about raising your children to be lovers of Christ rather than of the world. To press his point, he offers this principle: example is better than precept. Put differently, modeling and mentoring is more effective than lecturing—and even nagging! Murray writes on the power of example in parenting,

> Not in what we say and teach, but in what we *are* and *do*, lies the power of training. Not as we *think* as an ideal for which to train our children, but as *we live* do we train them. It is not our wishes or our theory, but our will and our practice that really train. It is by living the Christ-life that we prove that we love it, that we

have it; and thus will influence the young mind to love it and to have it too.[4]

Andrew Murray has captured what I take to be one of the main lessons of this passage in Titus: that example is better than precept, that we need to leverage relationships for the purpose of modeling and mentoring so we can teach others how to live the Christian life.

RECOGNIZE THE GOSPEL'S REPUTATION IS AT STAKE IN OUR TEACHING

Our third and final thesis is this: *our churches need to recognize that the gospel's reputation is at stake in our teaching.* One of the themes we've stressed in this book is that the good works of believers are for the sake of outsiders. Or more simply put, good works are evangelistic in their thrust.

We find that theme played out in this passage. If we fail to teach what accords with sound doctrine, we will inevitably fail to live lives that accord with sound doctrine. And if we fail to live lives that accord with sound doctrine, we will tarnish the reputation of the gospel. Or as Paul says, we will bring reproach on the Word of God (v. 5).

Similarly, he warns Titus several verses later that Titus himself must live out and teach what accords with sound doctrine "so that an opponent may be put to shame, having nothing evil to say about us" (v. 8). On the other hand, teaching what accords with sound doctrine in order to live lives that accord with sound doctrine will, put positively, "adorn the doctrine of God our Savior" (v. 10).

We don't often think of our behavior "adorning" our teaching. But that's precisely what Paul is saying. Teaching what accords with sound doctrine is one of the best means of evangelism. Do you want to reach the lost? Teach what accords with sound doctrine.

I find this ironic because Christians sometimes will pit discipleship against evangelism, as though they move in opposite directions. We tend to view discipleship as helping Christians go deep and move inward, while evangelism is obviously all about the church looking outside itself. But this passage reminds us that discipleship—or teaching—and evangelism shouldn't be seen as pulling in opposite directions. Instead, our teaching, and our modeling and mentoring, can have the powerful effect of commending the beauty of the gospel to outsiders.

Perhaps, then, we should think of this as a kind of *discipleship-evangelism*: to make disciples who know how to follow Jesus with their lives and thus know how to commend the gospel to outsiders.

As a pastor, I regularly receive some flyer or email about an upcoming conference intended to help ministry leaders be more effective at leading their churches in ministry and mission. Recently, I received an especially impressive-looking brochure for an upcoming conference. It was full of striking pictures and promising-sounding keynote addresses. In fact, I knew and liked several of the speakers on the docket.

But as I read about the topics this conference would address, I noted the conspicuous absence of anything even remotely approaching what we find here in Titus 2. So I began imagining myself offering a keynote address at this conference and asking the large assembly of those gathered to "turn in your Bibles to Titus chapter 2." And then I envisioned myself waxing eloquent on the fact that if the church really wants to advance the gospel in today's culture, then older men must live dignified lives, older women must live reverent lives, younger women must love their husbands and children, and younger men must get a grip on their passions and live self-controlled lives.

How do you suspect that might go over? I don't suspect that I'd receive a return invitation. But that's not because the advice isn't either biblical or missional. Instead, it's because it would likely be viewed as "out of touch," "old fashioned," or even "hard."

Let me tweak a line from G. K. Chesterton: it's not that the Bible's approach has been tried and found wanting. It's that the Bible's approach has been found difficult and therefore left untried.[5] It's very easy these days to stir up enthusiasm for technique. It's much harder to train people to renounce ungodliness and worldly passions, and to live self-controlled, upright, and godly lives in the present age (Titus 2:12). But we know which, in the long run, is truer to the gospel and more effective for gospel outreach.

CONCLUSION

Because the next passage in Titus and the next chapter in this book focus our gaze on *grace*, it's crucial that we end this chapter on this grace note. I suspect some will be inspired to come away from this chapter with a renewed sense of commitment and perhaps even a fresh set of plans for how to revise the teaching ministry of your church. That would be great. But we must remember that it is the grace of God that trains us in the art of living Christianly in the world. It is reliance upon what God has done, not what we do; it is resting in His provision for us, not the provisions we make for ourselves; it is looking to His Spirit for empowerment, not to ourselves for the motivation to do what needs to be done.

Unless we look to the grace of God and promote the grace of God in all our teaching, we may well end up in the predicament in which the Pharisees in Jesus' day found themselves. They were a well-disciplined bunch of teachers, but they were miles from the kingdom of God because they didn't understand the grace of God.

Teaching is vital in the life of the church. Next to preaching and good and godly leadership, it is the most important way in which we become a people who are zealous for good works. Why? Because solid, sound, practical teaching catalyzes our zeal for good works into the actual practice of good works. Yet the congregation is responsible for participating in the task of teaching. It's a calling placed upon each and every Christian. We should devote ourselves, and equip our churches, to be about the business of teaching what accords with sound doctrine. And it is grace that empowers us to that. Let's see how.

CHAPTER 5

What God Does Matters More

In this chapter, we turn our attention to the fourth element designed to mobilize your church for effective gospel outreach. Perhaps this chapter should have been the first. I say this for a simple reason: *what God does is more important than what we do.*

In our exposition of Titus, we've been looking at how the church ought to prioritize her ministries and organize herself for more effective gospel outreach. We've been flying under the banner of being *zealous for good works,* the catchphrase that comes from the passage of Scripture we'll consider in this chapter: Titus 2:11–14.

So far we've looked at three critical practices for the church: preaching (1:1–4), leadership (1:5–16), and teaching (2:1–10). These are three indispensable priorities and practices for any church that's serious about gospel outreach and committed to being a congregation zealous for good works. We can't be a city on a hill without biblical preaching, godly leadership, and sound teaching.

But despite how vital these three practices are for raising up a people who are zealous for good works, they ultimately are not the most important elements. They are not the most important because *we* are not the most important—God is! So as we think about how to be that city on a hill that Jesus describes, or how to become a people zealous for good works, we must remember that what God does is more important than what we do.

But what is it that God does that could be more important than all these practices we're called to? We can summarize our answer in one precious word—*grace*. God does grace. And that's what God *alone* can do. He alone gives grace. And grace is what we need most. And grace is ultimately what makes a congregation zealous for good works.

Grace is what this next passage in Titus is all about. So we're going to explore grace and celebrate grace by asking three questions of this passage. First, what is grace? Second, what does grace do when it appears? And third, what do we need to do to receive this grace?

WHAT IS GRACE?

The first question every Christian needs to answer, whether a pastor or layperson, is, *What is grace*? To answer this question, let's first establish a definition of grace and then explore a few characteristics of grace.

Many of us often talk about the grace of God as God's "unmerited favor" or God's favorable attitude toward us.

These are accurate and helpful definitions. But they, like most definitions, tend to be too abstract. The grace of God, as we learn from 2:11, is not an *abstraction* but an *action*.

According to the New Testament, grace is not merely an idea, but an act. Grace is not simply something God thinks or feels, but something God does. Grace, as this verse says, both appears and brings with it something immeasurably valuable. "For the grace of God has appeared, bringing salvation for all people" (v. 11).

Grace is an actual event in space and time: "the grace of God has appeared." Against every expectation, the grace of God shows up in human history and in our lives.

Grace is thus always surprising. No one could have anticipated grace's appearance. And grace is always sovereign. Grace appears not by human design or ingenuity, but by God's design and plan.

But what does it mean that grace "appeared, bringing salvation"? When did it appear, and how did it appear? In verse 14, Paul describes this grace that appeared by connecting it to the appearance and action of Jesus Christ, who, he says, "gave himself for us." Here, then, we are able to establish a working definition of *grace*. *Grace* is the self-giving of our God and Savior Jesus Christ for us.

In other words, *grace has a face*—and that face is the face of our great God and Savior Jesus Christ. That face is a scarred face, a bloody face, a dying face. That face is the face that agonized on the cross for your sins and mine. But that face is the face of grace. That is the face that has appeared, bringing salvation for all people.

Verse 14 also gives us several characteristics of grace,

telling us what grace is like. First, grace is *powerful*. The grace that appeared, the self-giving of our Savior, "redeem[s] us from all lawlessness." Just as God redeemed Israel from Egyptian bondage with a mighty, outstretched arm, so too the Son of God redeems, with great power, a new-covenant people from Egyptian-like bondage to lawlessness and sin. For only the grace of God in the death of His Son can redeem from lawlessness, can liberate from sin, can set the captive soul free. Nothing else will. Nothing else can.

We also learn from verse 14 that grace is *purifying*. Grace not only rescues and redeems but also purifies, cleanses, washes, renews. Our Savior gave Himself for us to redeem us and "to purify for himself a people." The grace of God that has appeared is purifying grace. The death of Christ cleanses. Later in Titus, we read about this aspect of grace again: "he saved us . . . by the washing of regeneration and renewal of the Holy Spirit" (3:5). Grace purifies our hearts by faith and our lives by the Holy Spirit.

The third characteristic of grace we see from verse 14 is that it is *possessive*. This is one of the more fascinating, even paradoxical, features of grace. For even though grace is incredibly generous, it is also tremendously possessive. You might even say that it is jealous. When grace comes into your life, it takes over. When grace enters in, it owns you. Grace buys you and makes you its own. And that's a very, very good thing. That's salvation.

So when you encounter the grace of God in the cross of Christ, you become no longer your own but "his own possession." Grace is possessive because it is costly. It cost God the life of His own Son.

But we must also understand that grace is not a onetime deal. Grace doesn't just appear and then disappear. No, grace is ongoing. Grace is, of course, embodied in the self-giving of the Son. But the Son continues to give Himself to His people, over and over again. The grace of the cross and the Son are always there—and always given afresh. Or as we learn from the prophet Jeremiah, "The steadfast love of the LORD never ceases; his mercies never come to an end; they are new every morning" (Lam. 3:22–23).

That's why Paul can encourage Timothy: "You then, my child, be strengthened by the grace that is in Christ Jesus" (2 Tim. 2:1). Or why Paul can say to the Corinthian church, "And God is able to make all grace abound to you, so that having all sufficiency in all things at all times, you may abound in every good work" (2 Cor. 9:8). Grace has appeared climactically in human history in the Son's death on the cross. But grace is always there for us in the continual self-giving of the Son, like a steady, never-ending stream.

WHAT DOES GRACE DO?

So we've answered our first question. *The grace of God is the self-giving of the Son for our salvation.* But what does grace do when it appears? What does grace do when it shows up in human history? Or what does it do when it shows up in human lives? We've answered this in part by looking at three characteristics of grace: it redeems, purifies, and possesses us. But let's dig deeper.

When grace appears, it gets straight to work and wastes no time. When grace shows up in our lives, it *trains us:*

"For the grace of God has appeared, bringing salvation for all people, *training* us to renounce ungodliness and worldly passions, and to live self-controlled, upright, and godly lives in the present age" (Titus 2:11–12, emphasis added). Grace, thank God, doesn't flatter us but trains us. It doesn't tell us all is well, but speaks bluntly and directly. Grace tells us that our lifestyle is suicidal, that we are a hundred and fifty pounds overweight, we smoke three packs of cigarettes per day, our blood pressure is off the charts, and we have a long family history of the worst kind of coronary disease, so to speak. And grace tells us what we need to do to change. Grace is less like a gentle counselor and more like a firm but loving coach. Grace undertakes to educate us, to train us, to run us through the paces, to reform and indeed transform.

Like all physical training, training in grace is for the purpose of living. Grace trains us in how to live better lives—how to live according to God's priorities and standards, not our own. Or, as Paul says in verse 12, grace trains us to live a certain kind of life, to live in a particular way, defined by particular character qualities. In this verse, Paul singles out three: first, grace trains us to develop self-control, a favorite theme in this letter and elsewhere in the Pastoral Epistles; second, grace trains us to live uprightly; and third, grace trains us to live godly lives. And it teaches and trains us in how to live, not for some other place and some other time, but for the *now-time*, this present age, which is precisely when we so desperately need the training of grace.

Paul doesn't elaborate on exactly how grace trains us to live a new life. We need the rest of the book of Titus, indeed the rest of the Bible, to flesh that out properly. Hebrews 12 is particularly helpful in this regard. There, we see that the training talked about here is actually divine discipline, and that the discipline God sends our way is difficult circumstances. We shouldn't therefore fuss or fret when challenges come our way, for they are fatherly discipline, training in grace:

> It is for discipline that you have to endure. God is treating you as sons. For what son is there whom his father does not discipline? If you are left without discipline, in which all have participated, then you are illegitimate children and not sons. Besides this, we have had earthly fathers who disciplined us and we respected them. Shall we not much more be subject to the Father of spirits and live? For they disciplined us for a short time as it seemed best to them, but he disciplines us for our good, that we may share his holiness. For the moment all discipline seems painful rather than pleasant, but later it yields the peaceful fruit of righteousness to those who have been trained by it. (Heb. 12:7–11)

So if you feel like the circumstances of your life are stretching you beyond what you think you can, or at least what you would want, to bear, then it may well be the grace of God training you. It's like you're at the gym and God is taking you through a serious workout. Yes, it hurts. No discipline is pleasant at the time. However, if you recognize it as grace and embrace it for what it is, then it will have that wonderful strengthening, fruit-producing effect in your life.

So don't chafe at the training of grace. Embrace it.

HOW DO WE EMBRACE
THE TRAINING OF GRACE?

How do we do that? Yes, grace trains us, but the training requires some degree of cooperation or response on our part. Anyone who's been to the gym or worked with a trainer has learned this unhappy lesson: you can't just show up for training and watch the trainer do all the work and somehow be benefited by it. No, you've got to actively engage, actively participate in the training if you're going to be changed by it.

In this passage, Paul identifies two critical steps we need to take in order to be trained by grace, for grace to have its proper effect in our lives. The life that grace trains us to live is, in this passage, literally flanked on both sides by the means of grace—what we must do, what steps we must take, to be trained by this grace. We must, first of all, *deny ourselves*. And second, we must *wait* for what we hope for. And yet even self-denial and hope-filled waiting are the expressions of God's grace in our lives. It is all of grace, from first to last.

Like physical training, training in grace requires that we take a critical and often difficult first step. That first step is self-denial. No one ever trains for a marathon who doesn't first begin saying no to various habits in their life that would otherwise get in the way of their preparing for the race. I know this because one of my closest friends from college invited me to join him and several other college friends in California several years ago for the San Francisco Marathon. But it didn't take me long to say no to the invitation. Why?

Because I knew I'd have to give up so much to engage in the training that was required. He sent me a training plan—weeks and weeks of running, hours and hours every week. Counting the cost and what I had to give up to make that happen, I simply said no.

Training in grace is like training for a marathon. If I had agreed to run the marathon with my friends, I would have had to say a different kind of no—no to various habits and routines. When it comes to training in grace, we have to say no to several things as a first step in the process. Paul identifies two—"ungodliness and worldly passions." Commenting on this passage, Calvin refers to these as "the two obstacles that chiefly hinder us" in our worship of God.[1] Ungodliness is whatever attitudes or actions that undermine God's centrality in your life. If it makes God marginal, it's ungodly. And worldly passions are the result of a hungry soul that doesn't have God at the center; passions for the things of the world ensue.

But, like training for a marathon, saying no to ungodliness and worldly passions is not a onetime act, just like saying no to sleeping in or taking a week off from running is not a onetime thing. No, it's an ongoing part of the training itself.

Yet here's the critical difference between training for a marathon and training in grace: the former lasts only several months or so, until the race is run and you're done. The latter, training in grace, lasts your whole life, or until *your race* is run and you're done. But until then, you're training, training in grace.

And so you're called to say no to or deny and renounce

any and every practice or pattern of life that gets in the way of the goal of the training. We're called to take up our cross—the cross of self-denial—every single day, as long as the Lord gives us breath.

The second critical step to take when training in grace is complementary yet counterintuitive—expectant waiting, which we read about in verse 13: "waiting for our blessed hope, the appearing of the glory of our great God and Savior Jesus Christ."

This verse provides a fitting complement to the call to deny oneself because it reminds us that self-denial is not a call to asceticism as an end in itself, but a call to position ourselves for something better, something greater, something even more glorious.

Waiting is also counterintuitive when it comes to training, for several reasons. First, we tend to think of waiting in primarily passive terms. If I'm waiting, I'm not working. How then can I be training if I'm waiting? But, biblically speaking, waiting is not passive. It's active.

In fact, waiting has a way of drawing us forward into action rather than causing us to sit back and relax. It does so because the object for which we wait is so attractive. Like a bridegroom waiting for his bride, there's nothing passive about waiting if the object is the chief object of one's desire.

I recently officiated a wedding and was able to watch a bridegroom wait for his bride, not least as she made that seemingly endless journey down the aisle to meet him at the front of the sanctuary. To see the look on his face, to sense the eagerness in his demeanor and the energy in his countenance—it was a waiting that, well, wasn't really waiting at all! Everything in him—his heart, his mind, his soul—was in motion, moving toward the object of his deepest desire.

This is the kind of waiting that corresponds with the object for which we wait: "our blessed hope, the appearing of the glory of our great God and Savior Jesus Christ" (v. 13). It is a *blessed* hope because, unlike every other hope we might have, it cannot be disappointed. Just as surely as Jesus Christ appeared for the first time, so too will He most assuredly appear for a second time.

Yet this time, He will not appear under the veil of frail humanity. He will be unveiled and fully glorified. Indeed, when He appears we shall see "the glory of our great God and Savior Jesus Christ." We shall see our *great God*—and yet, this great God will be, to those who know and love Him, a *Savior* who died in our stead. And this is the essence of the glory that we shall see: the greatness of God combined with the mercy of a Savior.

As we make good on these two means of grace—self-denial and expectant hope—we will find grace training us.

EMBRACE GRACE

There is nothing like grace that can revolutionize a life, nothing like grace that can turn people into zealots for good works. And our aim in this chapter has been to explore and to celebrate the surprising and sovereign grace of God.

Grace has appeared on the scene of human history, in the face of Jesus Christ. All that remains is to ask ourselves: Has grace appeared in my life? Have I embraced grace? And am I now living a life defined by grace?

How would you know if it has appeared in your life? You would know by seeing the effects of grace in your life. Grace is a mighty doer, a power, indeed, a person. Grace has a face. And when grace appears in your life, grace doesn't leave you unchanged but begins to transform you from the inside out.

We all need grace, every one of us. And not just once, but continually. We need a steady supply of the grace of God in our lives. Pray for grace to appear. Expect grace to appear. Look for grace to appear. And when it does, give thanks for the grace that has appeared. Because good works are bound to follow.

CHAPTER 6

Stop, Look, and Listen

How did an insignificant Jewish sect end up conquering the entire Roman world? How did the tiny Jesus movement of the first century end up transforming Western civilization for two millennia? In his book *The Rise of Christianity*, historian Rodney Stark explores these questions. One of the more fascinating chapters in the book deals with how the earliest Christians responded to plagues and epidemics.

In AD 165 and then again in AD 251, a plague swept through the empire, leaving a massive death toll in its wake. Stark describes two epidemics that hit the Roman world in the third century. They were devastating in terms of loss of life. But they were also deeply disorienting to the political and religious leaders of the day. They had no answers, no ready response to the crisis.

The Christians did, however. A church leader named Dionysius writes of the Christian response,

> Most of our brother Christians showed unbounded love and loyalty, never sparing themselves and thinking

only of one another. Heedless of danger, they took charge of the sick, attending to their every need and ministering to them in Christ, and with them departed this life serenely happy; for they were infected by others with the disease, drawing on themselves the sickness of their neighbors and cheerfully accepting their pains. Many, in nursing and curing others, transferred their death to themselves and died in their stead.[1]

What helped transform this insignificant Jewish sect into a transforming force was *readiness*. The earliest Christians were ready for every good work. As they saw needs around them, they responded with the love of Christ.

Titus 3:1–7 touches on this important aspect of being zealous for good works. Being zealous for good works requires a readiness for good works. Before we can be people that radiate the love of Christ through our lives, we need to be ready—willing and eager to respond to gospel opportunities that come across our path.

Readiness is an attitude that makes believers responsive to the needs around them. It's a state of mind, or a disposition; it's about being mentally and emotionally predisposed to respond with grace when an opportunity arises. It's about being available, prompt to react when you see a need that the love of Christ can address. The world is full of examples of the kind of readiness this passage talks about. We see mothers exude readiness as they beckon their toddler to take those first steps across the room; we see outfielders display readiness when a .300 batter steps up to the plate. They're ready to respond.

This passage in Titus unpacks several key elements regarding readiness: the call to readiness (vv. 1–2), the threat to readiness (v. 3), and the source of readiness (vv. 4–7).

THE CALL TO READINESS:
OUR CIVIC AND SOCIAL RESPONSIBILITY (3:1–2)

We are to be ready for every good work in two ways. First, we are to be ready for every good work in our *civic* responsibilities. When it comes to being a citizen within a community, Titus reminds the Christians in Crete that they are "to be submissive to rulers and authorities, to be obedient, to be ready for every good work" (v. 1).

We've heard of "civil disobedience." Here Titus calls for civil obedience. Civil obedience is to be the default position for the Christian. Consider Romans 13:1: "Let every person be subject to governing authorities." Or 1 Peter 2:13: "Be subject for the Lord's sake to every human institution." Of course, this does not mean blind subservience to anything and everything a government might do, since our allegiance is ultimately to God and not to man. But it does mean that Christians are to be good citizens—not political agitators or rabble-rousers or troublemakers. Instead, we are to be actively engaged in the life of our community so we can be "ready for every good work."

We are also to be ready for every good work in our *social* responsibilities—that is, we are to be ready to do good, not harm, to those with whom we live and work, to those we see out on the street or at the park or in our schools. This passage says we are "to speak evil of no one, to avoid quarreling, to be gentle, and to show perfect courtesy toward all people" (v. 2).

We've all met quarrelsome Christians, and they're usually not very attractive people. Quarrelsome Christians are those who love a good fight. They're grumpy and easily upset by most everything that happens. "The world's going to hell in a handbasket," is their mantra. "Turn or burn," is their bumper sticker. These kinds of people are looking for a fight, preferably with some surly pagans, so they can "stand up for Jesus." They like to argue with non-Christians. They like to put people in an apologetic headlock to see whether they can get them to say, "Uncle!"

Christians shouldn't be like that. Rather, we are to be good neighbors. To be sure, this is not a call to be weak-kneed or wimpy, to be a kind of Mr. Christian Milquetoast. Instead, it's a call to exhibit a remarkable amount of self-control and strength, the kind Jesus Christ exhibited as He interacted with the poor and the oppressed, the blind and the lame, the sick and the sinner.

In short, a Christian is to be a good citizen and a good neighbor. We are to be exemplary in our civic duties and social responsibilities. We are to be ready for every good work, whether it is in serving the needs of the society in which we live or the neighborhood in which we live. In the words of the prophet Jeremiah to the exiles of Israel, "But seek the welfare of the city where I have sent you into exile, and pray to the LORD on its behalf, for in its welfare you will find your welfare" (29:7). This adorns the doctrine of God our Savior.

We have many members of our congregation that seek to make Christ known by serving our local community in various ways. Most do this in very simple yet significant ways, whether as youth soccer coaches, members of the local PTA, or volunteers at the public library. You don't need to run for mayor to have an impact for Christ. Accessible opportunities abound in every community, yours included.

THE THREATS TO READINESS: OUR SINFUL ATTITUDES (3:3)

We are called to be ready for every good work. That's both our civic and social responsibility—and one way we live out our calling as a city on a hill in our local community.

But there are threats to readiness, aren't there? There are impediments to readiness, attitudes that make being ready for every good work more difficult, and indeed sometimes impossible. What are some of these attitudes that undermine readiness?

One is *ignorance*. We are simply unaware of the needs and opportunities around us and, therefore, fail to be ready for every good work. Or we may recognize the needs and opportunities, but we don't know how to meet them. Ignorance can thus stymie readiness for serving others. Our congregation learned this lesson the hard way. Several years ago, we wanted to do more for the most vulnerable children in our community. So we began to pray and look for opportunities. Then, to our own embarrassment, we realized that in our church's own backyard was a group home for neglected and abused children. Somehow, sadly, we had been ignorant of its presence. Thankfully, we remedied this and now enjoy a wonderful partnership with this important social service agency in our community. But we first had to confront our own ignorance before we could express Christ's kindness.

Another threat to readiness is *fear*. We may see the needs around us and even recognize them as good gospel opportunities, but for whatever reason, we're fearful of stepping out to meet the need—fearful of what it might cost us or fearful of how others might respond. This can sometimes happen when more affluent suburban churches fail to engage the needs of those in more urban and less affluent neighboring communities. Our church in Oak Park borders one of Chicago's most crime-ridden neighborhoods. It's only natural to be concerned for one's personal safety. But sometimes that can hinder us from serving our neighbors with Samaritan-like sacrificial love, regardless of the cost.

A third threat is *disdain*. Disdain is that subtle feeling of superiority toward others—feeling smug because you see yourself as better than others, feeling slightly exalted over others because of who you are or who you've become or what you've done or not done. Disdain is an ugly attitude nonetheless. Consider how John Calvin explains disdain:

> If there are any faults in others, not content with noting them with severe and sharp reproach, we hatefully exaggerate them. Hence arises such insolence that each one of us, as if exempt from the common lot, wishes to tower above the rest, and loftily and savagely abuses every mortal man, or at least looks down upon him as an inferior.[2]

More importantly, disdain is deadly. It kills zeal for good works. When we feel disdain toward someone, it's impossible to serve that person. And when we feel disdain toward whole groups of people, it's impossible to serve them. Disdain deadens our desire to serve and bless others. Yet we often struggle with disdain toward others, don't we?

But watch how this passage in Titus speaks to our attitudes of disdain toward others. Notice the flow of thought from verses 1–2, with their call for readiness, to verse 3, which introduces the reason why we ought to be ready for every good work. And what is that reason? "For we *ourselves* were once foolish, disobedient, led astray, slaves to various passions and pleasures, passing our days in malice and envy, hated by others and hating one another" (v. 3, emphasis added).

Did you follow the train of thought? Be ready for every good work (vv. 1–2) because of who you were (v. 3). In other words, being ready for every good work begins with a reminder of who we used to be. *Our readiness starts with remembering who we once were apart from Christ.* It's as if Scripture is saying, "If you want to be a good citizen and good neighbor, or a force for good in your community, then you must remember where you came from—the pit out of which the Lord rescued you!"

Rather than looking with disdain on the sin and rebellion and foolishness of the world around us, we ought to let it serve as a mirror in which we see our own reflection before we met Christ. In turn, this ought to drive us deeper and deeper into the grace of God, rather than higher and higher into our own superiority or self-righteousness.

There's nothing uglier than a smug Christian—a Christian who looks with disdain on sinners. In fact, it's a contradiction in terms. A smug Christian is a Christian who does not understand the grace of the gospel. A self-righteous Christian is a Christian whose heart has not been plowed by the tender mercies of God in Christ.

Here, as in all matters, Jesus Christ Himself is our supreme model. Jesus never looked with disdain on sinners. Jesus didn't despise sinners but had compassion on them (Mark 6:34). He didn't speak evil of sinners but rebuked the evil in their lives (John 7:53–8:11). He didn't quarrel with sinners but with Satan who takes people captive to do his will (2 Tim. 2:26).

Jesus was not harsh but gentle with the spiritually sick. Jesus was not gruff or rude or curt or impatient with the lowly, but "show[ed] perfect courtesy toward all people" (Titus 3:2)—indeed, even to His enemies. In fact, Jesus, "who, though he was in the form of God, did not count equality with God a thing to be grasped, but emptied himself, by taking the form of a servant, being born in the likeness of men. And being found in human form, he humbled himself by becoming obedient to the point of death, even death on a cross" (Phil. 2:6–8).

THE SOURCE OF READINESS: GOD'S GRACIOUS SALVATION (3:4–7)

But how do we deal with disdain in our hearts? And how do we become ready for every good work? This leads to our third point—*the source of readiness, which is God's gracious salvation.*

Like every right attitude in the Christian life, readiness for good works comes from being rooted in the gospel.

Our being ready for every good work depends upon our lives being firmly planted in the soil of God's gracious work in Christ.

Few verses in the Bible underscore the gracious character of God's salvation better or more clearly than this passage in Titus. In these packed verses, we're treated to a wonderfully succinct summary of the whole of salvation—a mini-theology on the doctrine of salvation. We see the source, the basis, the means, and the goal of salvation. And it's all about grace!

These verses unpack for us the gracious character of God's salvation in Christ.[3] And they begin where they ought, with the *source* of our salvation—which is ultimately the gracious character of our great God. "But when the goodness and loving kindness of God our Savior appeared, he saved us" (v. 4).

God sent His Son into the world not because the world is so special, but because God is so gracious. We often get this wrong. We often go to a verse like John 3:16 and think that it's because God "so" loved the world that He decided to save the world. But that's not the point of that verse. The point of that verse is to explain the *way in which* God saved the world: by sending His own Son. Put another way, God loved the world by sending His Son to die for the world.

The point is that salvation is rooted in God's character, not the lovability of the world. God didn't send His Son to save the world because the world is so loveable that He couldn't live without us. No, He saves us as an expression of His *goodness and loving-kindness,* not of our worth or value.

Paul continues to press home this point when he speaks

of the *ground* of salvation in verse 5: "not because of works done by us in righteousness, but according to his own mercy." God did not save you because of who you were. Nor, however, did He save you because of who you would become. Some of us have come to believe that we were a "good catch" for God. Thus, we harbor the secret feeling that God knew what He was doing when He saved us because of how great we would become for God.

We see the grace of God's salvation in the *means* of salvation. God saved us by the most gracious of means: "by the washing of regeneration and renewal of the Holy Spirit" (v. 5b). Salvation is not merely an external act—something that happens outside of us, in heaven or in the mind of God. Salvation includes God doing something within us as well. And this further underscores the graciousness of the whole splendid miracle. God renews us by giving us His own presence, His Holy Spirit. And, as verse 6 reminds us, He was not miserly in giving us His presence. No, He poured out His Holy Spirit richly upon us—all of grace!

Finally, we see the gracious character of God's salvation in the *goal* of salvation. As verse 7 says, we're not simply "justified by his grace," but also justified for a purpose. As if the free justification of God were not enough, God has more and more grace to give. He justifies us so that "we might become heirs according to the hope of eternal life" (v. 7).

So we see here the utter graciousness of God's salvation. The source, the basis, the means, the goal—it's all of grace, sheer grace! "For by grace you have been saved through faith. And this is not your own doing; it is the gift of God, not a result of works, so that no one may boast" (Eph. 2:8–9).

But here's the point: It is this gracious salvation, when believed and embraced, that effectively roots out our arrogance as we confess that salvation is all of God—and not our own doing. And it is this gracious salvation that makes us ready for every good work.

READINESS STARTS RIGHT WHERE YOU ARE

But where do we begin, whether as individuals or as a church? The answer is to begin *right where you are.* Tim Keller offers sage advice: we should stop, look, and listen.[4] Stop—that is, put the breaks on our busyness, which keeps us always going and never pausing to consider the needs of others. Look—open your eyes to the people around you, to see them with Jesus' eyes of concern and compassion. Listen—listen to other people, what they struggle with, wrestle with, and worry about. But also listen to God, what He might be saying to you.

Amazing things happen when you stop, look, and listen. You'll begin to notice needs everywhere—opportunities galore to display the goodness of God through the good works that flow from God's gospel. Tim Keller writes,

> You will notice a multitude of needs. There is a college student who has had to drop out of school for lack of funds. Over here are numbers of elderly folk without sufficient support from children, who need transportation, friendship, and other aid. Turn in another direction and listen hard. You will hear single parents, divorced and widowed people, struggling financially

and emotionally to be "both mother and father" to children. . . .

Now see the families temporarily in need because a mother or father is sick or injured [or out of work]. Other families struggle under more permanent disabilities; one has a mentally [handicapped] child, another has a father forced to retire early due to a severe back ailment, another family has a mother with Alzheimer's disease. Then there are the terminally ill—families struck by cancer, leukemia, and other such maladies.[5]

May God help us to stop, look, and listen—so that we may be ready for every good work.

CHAPTER 7

Give Chief Attention to the Chief Things

I'd like to introduce you to someone you should know—John Ploughman. He's an ordinary guy who gives extraordinary advice to people like you and me. I should tell you, though, that he's not real but fictitious. He's the creation of the Prince of Preachers, Charles Spurgeon. John Ploughman is a literary figure created by Spurgeon to offer sensible, sage, and often witty advice to the church on matters of first importance.

One of Ploughman's best pieces of advice is, "Never stop a plough to catch a mouse." Ole' John explains, "Think of a man and a boy and four horses all standing still for the sake of a mouse! Think of having a great work in hand, and then leaving it to squabble over some petty little nothing. That's as nonsensical as burning down your house to get rid of a few cockroaches!"[1]

Sadly, John Ploughman's own minister thought that churches were often the worst offenders in this regard.

"John," his minister says, "if you were on the committees of some of our societies you would see this mouse-hunting done to perfection. Not only committees, but whole bodies of Christian people, go mouse-hunting." With a little nudge from John, the minister went on to elaborate:

> A society of good Christian people will split into pieces over a petty quarrel, or mere matter of opinion, while all around them the masses are perishing for want of the gospel. A miserable little mouse, which no cat would ever hunt, takes them off from their Lord's work. Again, intelligent men will spend months of time and heaps of money in inventing and publishing mere speculations, while the great field of the world lies unploughed. They seem to care nothing how many may perish so long as they can ride their hobbies. In other matters a little common sense is allowed to rule, but in the weightiest matters foolishness is sadly conspicuous. As for you and me, John, let us kill a mouse when it nibbles our bread, but let us not spend our lives over it. What can be done by a mousetrap or a cat should not occupy all our thoughts.

Obviously John Ploughman and his minister knew a few things about the importance of focus. And how important *focus* is for the church! It's all too easy for the church to get off message and distracted from her mission by a thousand other trifles. In John's words, it's easy for the church to be busy mouse-hunting when we've got whole fields to plow.

It's remarkably common for churches and church leaders

to get sidetracked with secondary things. Everyone who has served in the leadership of a local congregation knows just how easy this is. When you should be praying for the nations or mobilizing outreach into your neighborhood, you're arguing about changing service times or the brand of coffee being served after church. Or when you should be visiting the sick and counseling the downtrodden, you're squabbling over some accounting procedure or why the high school ministry moved it's meeting from Tuesday to Wednesday night. Examples could be multiplied endlessly. But the point is the same: churches are vulnerable to "mission drift," to losing track of the main thing, to getting off target and off focus.

In the previous chapter, we considered the importance of readiness. In this chapter, we look at the importance of focus. In the next chapter, we will reflect on the importance of devotion. So, to clarify, the logic of these three chapters is this: ready, aim, and fire! Be ready for every good work. Focus on the right priorities that encourage good works. And devote yourself to the actual doing of good works.

Focus, however, is the main point of Titus 3:8–11. None of us can shirk the call to be focused if we want to live a life that has impact for the gospel. Focus is a critical practice, a critical discipline, for any church that cares about being zealous for good works and effectively advancing the gospel.

But how do we maintain focus? There are three disciplines that enable focus, one positive, two negative. As is often the case when it comes to focus, what we avoid is often as important as what we do. The three disciplines in this passage are: first, hammer on the great truths of the gospel (3:8);

second, steer clear of quarrels that add nothing and go nowhere (3:9); and third, deal with those who stir up division (3:10–11).

HAMMER ON THE GREAT
TRUTHS OF THE GOSPEL (3:8)

This first discipline is *hammer on the great truths of the gospel*. And it comes from the first verse of our passage: "The saying is trustworthy, and I want you to insist on these things, so that those who have believed in God may be careful to devote themselves to good works" (3:8).

Here, at the beginning of this verse, Paul refers to a trustworthy saying, one of five trustworthy sayings in the Pastoral Epistles, and it points us back to the preceding context where we find the trustworthy saying defined. The trustworthy saying is found in verses 4–7, where Paul rehearses the great truths of the gospel:

> But when the goodness and loving kindness of God our Savior appeared, he saved us, not because of works done by us in righteousness, but according to his own mercy, by the washing of regeneration and renewal of the Holy Spirit, whom he poured out on us richly through Jesus Christ our Savior, so that being justified by his grace we might become heirs according to the hope of eternal life.

Now Paul says this is a trustworthy, reliable, rock-solid truth: our salvation is all of grace. But he also says to Titus that he is "to insist on these things," or to hammer away on these truths. Not in order to be tedious, but to encourage those who have actually come to know this God of grace to let their knowledge be active, not idle.

Titus is to insist on these things "so that those who have believed in God may be careful to devote themselves to good works" (v. 8). That's how stimulating zeal for good works happens: by maintaining singular focus on the great gospel truths of Scripture and by hammering away on these truths until they are driven deep into the soul of every man and woman and child. Which in turn is the way we adorn the doctrine of God our Savior (2:10). For good works, as our passage says, are not only "excellent" in their own right, but "profitable for people," inviting to outsiders.

So, don't neglect to preach and teach and sing and celebrate rich biblical truths like the unity of Father, Son, and Spirit; the sovereignty of God; the incarnation and virgin birth; the power of Christ's atoning blood; the new birth; regeneration; adoption; justification; reconciliation; the empowering presence of the Spirit; the hope of eternal life; and the promise of a new heavens and new earth. These core Christian convictions have a way of animating faith.

The great gospel truths of 3:4–7 are like a nail. Our responsibility as a church, then, is to hammer constantly on these great gospel truths. This is the starting point and the most important thing in staying focused—insisting on the great truths of the gospel. It's all too easy for the church to get "off message," to get distracted.

So, too, for each one of us. We too should on a daily basis be doing our own hammering, driving these truths deep into our own souls. Is it your daily practice to drive the gospel nail an inch or two deeper into your soul?

What this looks like in practice is making Christ ever and always central in all that we do and say. Proclaim Him—that's how Paul defined his mission and ministry and message (Col. 1:27). I love what Spurgeon says on this point: "Brethren, first and above all things, keep to plain evangelical doctrines; whatever else you do or do not preach, be sure incessantly to bring forth the soul-saving truth of Christ and him crucified."[2] This is precisely what Paul calls for in our passage: stay focused by hammering away on the great truths of the gospel, on Christ and Him crucified.

STEER CLEAR OF QUARRELS
THAT ADD NOTHING AND GO NOWHERE (3:9)

The first discipline reminds us what we must devote ourselves to, what we must insist on, what we must preach and teach and speak to one another. The second discipline, however, has to do with what we must avoid. The second discipline has to do with activities that are remarkably effective at distracting a church from her mission—quarrels and controversies.

As we saw earlier in the letter, in 1:10–16, there were some influential leaders in the churches in Crete teaching ideas they shouldn't be teaching and acting in ways they shouldn't be acting. They were from a Jewish background and putting great stock in legal matters related to the Jewish law.

But these, as Paul points out, were only breeding controversy and stirring up quarrels. So Paul forcefully yet kindly instructs Titus, "But avoid foolish controversies, genealogies, dissensions, and quarrels about the law" (3:9a). And if Titus should, so too should we. This is the second discipline for maintaining focus—*steer clear of quarrels that add nothing and go nowhere.*

Why is it so important to steer clear of foolish controversies? Because, Paul says, "they are unprofitable and worthless" (3:9). They don't advance the gospel, but distract from it. They add nothing and go nowhere. And they certainly don't stir up zeal for good works. Instead, they sap it. In addition, foolish controversies can become exceedingly harmful to churches, as too many of us are painfully aware. Listen to what Paul says to Timothy:

> Remind them of these things, and charge them before God not to quarrel about words, which does no good, but only ruins the hearers. Do your best to present yourself to God as one approved, a worker who has no need to be ashamed, rightly handling the word of truth. But avoid irreverent babble, for it will lead people into more and more ungodliness, and their talk will spread like gangrene. (2 Tim. 2:14–17)

So Paul says both to Titus and Timothy, and to us, that we are to avoid quarrels and foolish controversies—literally, to walk around them, to steer clear of them. We are to treat them like quicksand, because once you step into them, you'll have a very difficult, if not impossible, time getting out—and all your energy and attention will be absorbed. We are to avoid them.

But an important qualification is in order at this point. Not all controversy is foolish. Nor is all debate pointless. Frankly, in our social media–saturated world, it's sometimes difficult to distinguish between substantive controversies and those that are silly. Twitter and twenty-four-hour news-feeds have a way of making every little flare-up seem like a historic event. But so much of this is episodic in meaning and unworthy of the church's sustained attention. It's often best to turn one blind eye and one deaf ear to these passing tempests.

But sometimes controversy is necessary and even beneficial for the church. In the epistle of Jude, for example, we are told "to contend for the faith that was once for all delivered to the saints" (v. 3). Or think of Paul's letters, everyone one of which is contending for some truth and engaged in refuting some form of error or heresy. The same could be said of Jesus Himself. Did you realize that there wouldn't be a church if the church did not engage in controversy to preserve and protect the doctrine of the church? And did you realize that there would be no New Testament if believers were to avoid any and *all* controversy, since much of the New Testament is written to deal with particular points of doctrine and practice?

We're not called to avoid any and all controversy. Instead, we're called to avoid a certain kind of controversy— *foolish* controversy. But how do you distinguish between the two—controversy that serves the church and controversy that distracts the church? How can you tell the difference between fruitful controversy, on the one hand, and foolish controversy, on the other? Here are a few principles that will help you know when it's a foolish rather than a fruitful controversy:

First, you know it's a foolish controversy when you find yourself quarreling over a minor doctrinal point as though it were a major truth of the faith. This is perhaps the most common temptation, since we all have our own doctrinal hobbyhorses we like to ride. For some of us, it's easy to make a mountain of controversy out of a molehill of doctrine. And we want to persuade others that this particular issue—*our* issue—really is of first importance for the church.

The reality is that while some doctrines are indeed primary and must be believed by Christians, there are plenty of doctrines that are secondary and even tertiary, about which Christians can amicably agree to disagree. The Trinity, the deity of Christ, the necessity of the cross, the bodily return of Jesus—these are primary. But the mode of baptism, the timing of the rapture, or the style of worship—these are secondary and even tertiary matters. Christians shouldn't normally spend too much energy debating these.

Listen to Charles Spurgeon's sage advice on this point.

> Do not make minor doctrines main points. Do not paint the details of the background of the gospel picture with the same heavy brush as the great objects in the foreground of it. For instance, the great problems of sublapsarianism and supralapsarianism, the trenchant debates concerning eternal filiation, the earnest dispute concerning the double procession, and the pre or post millenarian schemes, however important some may deem them, are practically of very little concern

to that godly widow woman, with seven children to support by her needle, who wants far more to hear of the loving-kindness of the God of providence than of these mysteries profound; if you preach to her on the faithfulness of God to his people, she will be cheered and helped in the battle of life; but difficult questions will perplex her or send her to sleep. She is, however, the type of hundred of those who most require your care.[3]

Second, you know it's a foolish controversy when you engage in debate or dispute in the wrong way or with the wrong methods—when you find yourself attacking someone else's character or questioning their Christian commitment because they happen to disagree with you. In other words, a worthwhile debate can become a foolish controversy when we act like fools.

Third, you know it's a foolish controversy when you debate for the wrong reasons or with the wrong goals in mind. If it's a critical issue and you care about the health of the church, then the controversy can often be constructive and fruitful. But if your primary concern is to win an argument, score points on someone else, or show your skillfulness in debate, then you are likely engaged in a foolish controversy.

Alternatively, fruitful controversy is controversy that is entered into with the right aims and intentions, in the right way, and over the right kinds of issues—genuinely important issues, issues that the history of the church has shown to be important, issues that Christians down through the ages have agreed are important. When all these elements are in place, then it can be fruitful controversy for the sake of the gospel and the purity and preservation of the church's witness in the world. For the sake of all the widows and other humble, godly servants of the Lord Jesus Christ who long only to be well fed upon the rich truths of God's Word and to hear of the goodness and loving-kindness of God our Savior, let us resolve to *steer clear of quarrels that add nothing and go nowhere, that neither illuminate nor edify, but only distract and demoralize.*

DEAL WITH THOSE WHO STIR UP DIVISION (3:10–11)

So these are the first two disciplines required for maintaining focus. But here's the challenge. Even if we as a church hammer on the great truths of the gospel and steer clear of quarrels that add nothing and go nowhere, we might still struggle with maintaining focus. Even if we do our part, there may yet be some in the church who are unwilling to do their part. There are those in every church who distract the church from her ministry and mission by stirring up division.

So the third and final discipline we need in order to maintain focus is *deal with those who stir up division.* This is what Paul calls Titus to do in the last two verses of this passage. He writes, "As for a person who stirs up division, after warning him once and then twice, have nothing more to do with him, knowing that such a person is warped and sinful; he is self-condemned" (3:10–11).

Who is a person that stirs up division? One whose primary interest is *power.* They want power in and thus influence over the church. But they seek to exert influence not with the tools of the Word and the Spirit and the gospel, but with three tools Paul refers to back in the first chapter: insubordination, empty talk, and deception (1:10). They are insubordinate to the Word of God and the leadership of the church; that's the starting point. But they will try to garner people to their cause with words, words, words—what Paul simply refers to as empty talk. And thus they are skilled in the art of deception. The end result is an attempt to accumulate power through the manipulation of relationships for personal gain. That's the profile of a person who stirs up division. And people like this, friends, kill churches. They split leadership and undermine authority and ultimately distract the church from her mission.

How do you deal with those who stir up division? You respond to them with discipline. That's what Paul describes in these verses, a three-stage process of church discipline. The first and second stages involve issuing the person with an informal or semiformal warning, clarifying that what the person is doing is divisive and admonishing them to turn away from his ways. At this point in the process, the goal is restoration, and the purpose of these two warnings is to accomplish that end. Further, the process is to be pursued with gentleness and grace and patience (see 2 Tim. 2:22–25).

But if the person is unwilling to renounce his ways, then the leadership is forced to advise the church to avoid or shun the person, to "have nothing more to do with him" (3:10). And when it comes time for us as a church to do that, we can do so with brokenhearted resolve, knowing that the person has already done it to themselves. This is the point of verse 11: take the final step of avoidance or shunning or disassociating with the person, "knowing that such a person is warped and sinful; he is self-condemned."

Now, it is important to note two things. First, the process Paul outlines here is strikingly similar to and perhaps even patterned after the process Jesus describes in Matthew 18 for dealing with sin:

> "If your brother sins against you, go and tell him his fault, between you and him alone. If he listens to you, you have gained your brother. But if he does not listen, take one or two others along with you, that every charge may be established by the evidence of two or three witnesses. If he refuses to listen to them, tell it to the church. And if he refuses to listen even to the church, let him be to you as a Gentile and a tax collector." (vv. 15–17)

The second thing you should know is that every church's leadership team should be committed to following this instruction. Yes, do it prayerfully and humbly and broken-heartedly, but do it. Churches must practice loving church discipline because the very integrity of our message and vitality of our mission depends upon it. Your church will never become a city on a hill without exercising church discipline.

GIVE CHIEF ATTENTION TO THE CHIEF THINGS

"Never stop a plough to catch a mouse." That's John Ploughman's good and godly advice to all of us who are engaged in the life and ministry of the church. And it matches these words we have from God's Word, words telling us we need focus.

We need gospel focus as a church. Focus is a critical discipline for the church because there's nothing like "doing church" to distract the church from her message and mission.

Staying focused requires hammering home the great truths of the gospel, in season and out of season; it requires steering clear of quarrels that add nothing and go nowhere; and it means we must, on occasion, deal with those who stir up division and thus distract the church from her mission.

Consider one final word from John Ploughman's minister, who for the benefit of us all rightly says:

> Let us give our chief attention to the chief things—the glory of God, the winning of souls for Jesus, and our own salvation. There are fools enough in the world, and there can be no need that Christian men should swell the number. Go on with your ploughing, John, and I will go on with my preaching, and in due season we shall reap if we faint not.[4]

May it be so for our churches! May we continue with our preaching and teaching and life together as communities of faith, giving our chief attention to the chief things, staying focused on the great truths of the gospel and turning aside from everything that would hinder or distract us from our great mission. For only by doing so will we be the kind of people who are zealous for good works.

CHAPTER 8

Devoted to Good Works

In his book *The Hole in Our Gospel*, Richard Stearns describes his transforming trip to Rakai, Uganda, in August of 1998. He movingly describes an encounter with a Ugandan also named Richard:

> His name was Richard, the same as mine. I sat inside his meager thatch hut, listening to his story, told through the tears of an orphan whose parents had died of AIDS. At thirteen, Richard was trying to raise his two younger brothers by himself in this small shack with no running water, electricity, or even beds to sleep in. There were no adults in their lives—no one to care for them, feed them, love them, or teach them how to become men. There was no one to hug them either, or to tuck them in at night. Other than his siblings, Richard was alone, as no child should be. I try to picture my own children abandoned in this kind of deprivation, fending for themselves without parents to protect them, and I cannot.

I didn't want to be there. I wasn't *supposed* to be there, so far out of my comfort zone—not in that place where orphaned children live by themselves in their agony.[1]

Just sixty days earlier, Stearns had been the CEO of Lenox, America's finest tableware company, which produces and sells millions of dollars in luxury goods. He writes of his life as a high-powered corporate CEO:

> I lived with my wife and five children in a ten-bedroom house on five acres just outside of Philadelphia. I drove a Jaguar to work every day, and my business travel took me to places such as Paris, Tokyo, London, and Florence. I flew first-class and stayed in the best hotels. I was respected in my community, attended a venerable suburban church, and sat on the board of my kids' Christian school. I was one of the good guys—you might say a "poster child" for the successful Christian life.[2]

But God got a hold of Stearns and eventually called him to resign his comfortable position as a corporate CEO to become the president of a global relief agency known as World Vision. God birthed in him what the book of Titus calls a devotion to good works.

How does that happen? How does a high-flying corporate executive like Richard Stearns become devoted to good works? Or how does someone like you or me become devoted to good works?

The final passage of Titus holds out the key, "And let our people learn to devote themselves to good works, so as to help cases of urgent need, and not be unfruitful" (3:14). Intriguingly, this is Paul's final appeal to Titus and to the churches in Crete. In it, we see Paul's apostolic heart for his churches—that they not be unfruitful but fruitful; that they not live humdrum, half-hearted lives, but lives that abound with good works and advance the gospel.

LEARNING BY DOING

We also see how this happens. It happens by *learning*. We avoid unfruitfulness by learning to devote ourselves to good works. "And let our people *learn* to devote themselves to good works," Paul writes (3:14, emphasis added).

Devotion to good works requires learning. It does not happen automatically. Devotion to good works is not our default setting. You don't come preprogrammed with a devotion to good works. Instead, devotion to good works is something that must be cultivated, learned.

But we learn to be devoted to good works not by signing up for a class on good works or by reading books about good works. We don't learn to be devoted to good works in that way, through an analysis of good works.

Instead, we learn to be devoted to good works *by doing good works*. In fact, the force of the verb here translated "learn" is more "to learn through practice,"[3] to learn through experience. We learn devotion to good works, then, by doing good works. Devotion to good works comes through our own firsthand experience of good works.[4]

Of course, this principle applies to virtually every area of life, as well as in every area of the Christian life. Praying develops devotion to prayer. Reading your Bible develops devotion to reading your Bible. Giving develops devotion to giving. Serving develops devotion to serving. Praising develops devotion to praising. In each case, we see the devotion follows the doing.

So, too, devotion to good works—it follows doing good works.

Vern Hendrickson was to me a great example of this principle. Vern was a member of our church for over forty years, and for most of that time, he served as our treasurer. Nearly four decades of faithful service and devotion to good works. In fact, I remember on one occasion, Vern was in the office doing payroll, then went to the dentist for a root canal, and then returned to church to finish signing checks! Vern was devoted to good works. But he had learned to be devoted to good works over many years of faithful service.

Jesus Christ is also an example of this principle. You may be surprised to hear that the Bible says that Jesus learned through experience, through doing. This is what the writer of Hebrews says: "he learned obedience through what he suffered" (5:8). Although He was the Son of God, He learned obedience through suffering. Even though He knew all things, He was able to learn from firsthand experience what it meant to obey the Father through suffering. Like Jesus, we too must learn to be devoted to good works through doing good works.

GOOD WORKS AND URGENT NEEDS

But what are good works? What makes a work a *good* work? Ironically, throughout this book on being zealous for good works, we have not paused to define good works. It's now high-time to do so! Here is a workable definition: *good works are human acts that meet gospel needs in the name of Jesus Christ.*

First, good works are human acts. They are not primarily dispositions or feelings or thoughts but are actions. Second, good works meet gospel needs. Good works address those needs that are exposed by the gospel; in other words, they serve to advance the gospel. Third, good works are done in the name of Jesus Christ. "Whatever you do, in word or deed, do everything in the name of the Lord Jesus" (Col. 3:17). Motivation is critical, and what makes a work a good work is the motivation to do it in Jesus' name, in a way that brings honor to Him.

Of course, this definition is broad enough to encompass good works of every size and shape and variety—from the mundane to the magnificent, from the humble to the Herculean. And that is good and right and biblical.

This passage does, however, specify that we are to learn to devote ourselves to good works, *so as to help cases of urgent need.* There are many needs. But this passage says we are to prioritize urgent needs. But which are the urgent ones, and which are not? And is it possible that I could think something is an urgent need when God doesn't see it that way at all? Or, conversely, is it possible that God thinks something is an urgent need, when I don't think it's urgent at all?

I remember early in my ministry at Calvary having lunch with a fellow Oak Park clergy member. Over the course of the conversation, this person asked whether we as a church would ever be interested in partnering together on some community projects. I responded that we were certainly open to that sort of thing, but asked what this person thought to be the urgent needs in the community. This person replied: affordable housing. Now, I have nothing against affordable housing. But before embarking on something like that, we would want to prayerfully consider whether that is an urgent *gospel* need. This doesn't mean it has to be explicitly evangelistic. But it should flow from and serve to promote the good news about Christ's death and resurrection.

What, then, defines an urgent need? Here is where the other verse in this passage helps us. In the original Greek of verse 14, there is an "also" (*kai*). It would have been helpful to have included this "also" in the translation so that it read, "Let our people *also* learn to devote themselves to good works." What this clarifies is that what Paul instructs Titus to do in 3:12–13 is an expression of what he instructs the churches to do in 3:14. In other words, just as the churches of Crete are to learn to devote themselves to good works to help cases of urgent need, so too this is what Paul instructs Titus himself to do—to devote himself to good works to help cases of urgent need.

In 3:12–13, Paul offers a variety of instructions about travel plans. But this all serves the single purpose of advancing the gospel. He's not interested in Titus joining him in Nicopolis for the winter to go snow skiing. No, he's deploying and redeploying Christian workers all over the Mediterranean for the sake of the advance of the gospel.

In fact, we see Paul's intentionality and missionary urgency coming through in these closing instructions. Paul calls Titus to join him in Nicopolis. Nicopolis was a large city located in western Macedonia on the Adriatic Sea, no doubt ripe for gospel outreach. There was no church in that city. It was also a city for strategic gospel work. From there, Paul could advance the gospel in Asia Minor. Nicopolis was "an ideal location for Paul to continue meeting people and spreading the gospel."[5] It would have been a good base of operations for him as he sought to advance the gospel farther west to Spain.

Paul says that Titus is to ensure that Zenas and Apollos receive a good send-off so that they lack nothing. The New Testament writings put great stress on the importance of a good send-off for Christian workers (see Acts 15:3; Rom. 15:24; 1 Cor. 16:6; 2 Cor. 1:16; 3 John 6). It included all kinds of financial and material support: food, clothing, travel arrangements, and companions. But these send-offs also included prayer and fasting (see Acts 13:3; 20:36–38; 21:5–6).

This presupposes that Titus would extend to them hospitality while they were in Crete. It also, of course, means that Titus is to see to it that they leave Crete not lacking anything they need. This would have included financial and material support and other practical helps. The phrase "lack nothing" is always used of Christian missionary efforts (see 3 John 6). As one commentator has noted, this is "a delicate allusion to the underwriting of their expenses."[6]

What, then, defines urgency? The gospel does. Good works that address cases of urgent need are those that advance the gospel. But does this mean that only missionaries or pastors or other Christian workers can do good works? No, because these are not the only ways in which the gospel is advanced in the world. Do you remember, for example, the word to slaves in 2:10? They are to adorn the doctrine of God our Savior by living exemplary lives in their work-world. There is an urgent need to advance the gospel in the marketplace, in the home, and in the neighborhood. So learn to devote yourselves to good works in those places.

A SERVING CHURCH

In closing, let me share a few important points to keep in mind when it comes to learning-by-doing or learning through experience. First, this kind of learning takes time. It doesn't happen overnight. It happens gradually.

Second, learning through experience requires patience. This is true of virtually all learning, but especially learning to devote yourself to good works.

Third, this kind of learning will inevitably be painful. Most learning is painful. It takes effort. It can be frustrating and fatiguing—all the more when learning devotion to good works. It will be painful because we will be learning something that doesn't come naturally to any of us: we are learning to be devoted to *other people* and *not ourselves*.

Finally, this kind of experiential learning is best done in community, with others who are going through the same process and where you are praying together.

One of the things that happens when you work through an entire book of the New Testament like Titus is that you begin to develop a vision for your own church. As we conclude our study on Titus, I want to share with you a dream I have for my church, and a dream I hope you (will) have for your church. It is a dream I heard shared by one of my heroes in the faith, John Stott. It's a dream of a serving church.

> I have a dream of a church which is *a serving church*— which has seen Christ as the Servant and has heard his call to be a servant too, which is delivered from self-interest, turned inside out, and giving itself self-lessly to the service of others, whose members obey Christ's command to live in the world, to permeate secular society, to be the salt of the earth and the light of the world, whose people share the good news of Jesus simply, naturally and enthusiastically with their friends, which diligently serves its own [community], residents and workers, families and single people, nationals and immigrants, old folk and little children, which is alert to the changing needs of society, sensitive and flexible enough to keep adapting its program to serve more usefully, which has a global vision and is constantly challenging its young people to give their lives in service, and constantly sending its people out to serve. I have a dream of a *serving* church.[7]

What a great dream for a church! That's my dream for my church, and I hope and pray that it's your dream for your church. And if we continue to learn to devote ourselves to good works, who knows what God might be pleased to do through us—exceedingly beyond all that we could ask or think!

A City on a Hill

This book began as a list that I had developed while fighting a head cold. A number of years ago, I was supposed to deliver a message at our church's biannual meeting. But instead, I spent the evening at home in bed sick, so much so that by Sunday evening our son Ezra asked whether I was trying to grow a mustache—I hadn't shaved in days!

Looking back I can say that the head cold and missing the meeting was God's good providence. It gave me an opportunity to reflect more deeply on what I had intended to share: the identity and calling of the church—not just our church, but *the* church.

But this book also began with a list. For the first sixth months of my ministry as the new senior pastor of Calvary Memorial Church in Oak Park, Illinois, where I served for a decade, I had been keeping a list of things I might address at this important all-church business meeting. By the time the meeting arrived, the list had grown to over eighteen items, with headings and subheadings! There was lots on my mind—and lots I wanted to share with our congregation.

As I thought about how to bring these ideas together into a single message, it became clear to me that dumping all my ideas on our congregation wasn't the best way forward. Nor did I think it made sense to take this opportunity to explain some of the recent changes that had taken place. Nor did I think this was the time to roll out a new strategic plan or five-year goals. Rest assured, these were just the things that had been on my mind. But as my dad likes to say, "Todd, timing is everything in life."

Instead, what I was compelled to share with our congregation was something both simpler and more profound than any of the aforementioned. I offered them one simple observation about our church, and then drew out one simple implication.

That was all. Yet this one observation is singularly important for the life and ministry of the church—not just our church, but *the* church. The observation is this: *the church of Jesus Christ, and each local expression of it, is a city on a hill.*

WHAT IS A CITY ON A HILL?

The followers of Jesus are a city on a hill. As many will recognize, I am alluding to the beginning of the Sermon on the Mount, where in that well-known portion of Matthew's gospel Jesus says to His disciples, "You are the light of the world. *A city set on a hill* cannot be hidden. Nor do people light a lamp and put it under a basket, but on a stand, and it gives light to all in the house" (Matt. 5:14–15, emphasis added).

It's worth noting that Jesus spoke these words *to His disciples.* They were intended to provide not only the motivation but a sense of identity to all who would follow after this King who had come in the flesh. So, these words apply to every one of you who have taken up your cross and are seeking to live your life in obedience to King Jesus. You are the light of the world; you are a city on a hill. That's who you are by virtue of your allegiance to Jesus; that's your identity.

But I also think Jesus' words apply to whole *groups*. Not just individuals, but whole groups of believers can be a city on a hill. We call that a church.

Jonathan Edwards, the great American pastor-theologian, helped me understand this. Over two hundred and fifty years ago, at the onset of the First Great Awakening, a time of remarkable spiritual revival in America, Edwards preached a sermon from Matthew 5:14 to his congregation in Northampton, Massachusetts, entitled, "A City on a Hill." In that sermon, he identifies three marks that characterize a church as a city on a hill:

1. *A church is a city on a hill if it has a distinct faith.* And this in one of two ways. A church can have a distinct faith because of *what* it teaches; and a church can have a distinct faith because of *how* it teaches what it teaches. The first has to do with the doctrine: What does the church believe? What is its doctrine? The second has to do with devotion: How intensely or fervently does it hold onto its beliefs? Of course, a church stands out as a city on a hill when it either preaches and teaches what other churches don't or

when it's willing to stake its life on its teaching in a way other churches won't—or both![1]

2. *A church is a city on a hill if God has done something distinct in it.* Here, Edwards is asking whether God has been at work in an unusual way within the life of the church. Is there evidence of God's hand of blessing in the life of the church? Do we have reason to think that God has poured out His grace in special measure upon a church? A church is a city on a hill, in Edwards's words, "when God appears in any very remarkable and very wonderful works amongst a people."[2]

3. *A church is a city on a hill if it, or any of its members, has a distinct influence on others.* "A professing society," writes Edwards, "is sometimes a city set on a hill on that account, by reason of the great and extensive influence that they have, or what is seen in them or heard of them has, on others."[3] Edwards is describing, in a word, *impact*. Has the church, or its members, had a significant impact on others? If so, it is a city on a hill, a church with a distinct impact on those around it.

IS YOUR CHURCH A CITY ON A HILL?

So these are the three marks of a church that is a city on a hill, at least according to Edwards. And it goes without saying that I agree with him on this point—naturally, otherwise I wouldn't be taking you down this path! Edwards gives us a great set of diagnostic questions. Let's take the first mark. Does your church have a distinct faith? Does your doctrine or your devotion to your doctrine cause you to stand out within your community and, in that sense, serve as a city on a hill?

But how about the second mark? Has God done something distinct in your church? Is there evidence of God's hand of blessing in the life of your congregation?

Finally, does your church or its members have a significant impact in the lives of others and in your community?

But if this is a valid definition of a city on a hill, then the question becomes, in my mind, and I trust in yours as well: Are *we* a city on a hill? Is *your church* a city on a hill? If so, then so what? And perhaps even more importantly, if *not*, then what? What can be done to help encourage and equip, to help motivate and mobilize, your church to be a city on a hill?

A PRIVILEGE TO BE
ENJOYED OR A DECISION TO BE MADE?

But what is the significance of all this? To be a city on a hill is not a privilege to be enjoyed. This is not some feather in our cap, something to take pride in or boast about. Much less is it something to begin advertising to the community with an ad, for example, in the *Wednesday Journal*: "Visit the only city on a hill in the western suburbs this Sunday." No, to be a city on a hill is not some status symbol to revel in or a privilege to enjoy.

To be a city set on a hill is also not a decision to be made. It's not something we resolve in our own minds to become or strive after, even though it's often thought of in that way. It's not a resolution to pass at a biannual meeting or a new ministry strategy to implement or a strategic goal.

Do you know the children's song "This Little Light of Mine"? That's a great, peppy song, isn't it? The only problem is that it misses the point of the biblical text. Jesus is quite emphatic about the fact that, as His follower, you *are* the light of the world; you *are* a city set on a hill. And, as He says, "A city set on a hill *cannot* be hidden" (Matt. 5:14, emphasis added). There's no hiding your light under a bushel, as though you can be a follower of Jesus and not let your light shine. Instead, the only two options are this: you either follow Jesus as a city on a hill and let your light shine, or you fail to follow Jesus.

Put positively, to be a city on a hill is *a calling to embrace* and *a responsibility to steward*. This is something *God does*, not us, and something God does *to us* and *through us*, not something we strive to be or do for ourselves. It is a reality by virtue of the sovereign call of God upon the life of this community and the sovereign work of God within this community. We simply are a city on a hill. And this means, as Jesus says, it is our responsibility, by virtue of this calling upon our life together as a church to "let [our] light shine before others, so that they may see [our] good works and give glory to [our] Father who is in heaven" (Matt. 5:16).

A city set on a hill—that's our calling as the church. And to let the light of our lives shine before others that they may see our good deeds and glorify God—that's our responsibility as the church.

How do we steward this calling and discharge this responsibility to the best of our ability? And how do we stir up the zeal for good works that turns churches into missional congregations that make a big impact for Jesus? The book of Titus—an ancient source of wisdom for the contemporary church, with seven practices that have the potential to energize any local congregation—has shown us the way. Preaching, leadership, teaching, grace, readiness, focus, and learning—there is nothing particularly novel here. But when these seven practices are embraced, great things can and indeed will happen for the kingdom.

Questions for Small Group Discussion

CHAPTER 2: WHAT TURNS A PLACE UPSIDE DOWN?

Biblical Text: Titus 1:1–4

First Reaction

1. What one aspect of this chapter do you hope we as a group would talk about?

2. Todd mentioned that hearing the Word of God preached should be the high point of your week. Is it the high point of your week? If not, what is?

Into the Word

1. Todd said the reason for preaching is God's own self-revelation. God is not silent. He has spoken and still speaks (see Titus 1:2–3 and 1 Peter 4:11). Do you come

to church with the expectation for God to reveal Himself to you?

2. Todd noted that the content of preaching is determined by the convictions of the people and the preacher. He said that preaching should be: (1) biblical, (2) expositional, and (3) Christ-centered. If preaching is to be expositional (defined as "letting the message of the text be the message of the sermon"), how would you define expositional listening?

3. How should expositional listening affect our convictions? How can it lead to worship?

4. The purpose of preaching is to bring out the knowledge of the truth that pulls back the veil of understanding, so that the light shines forth the glory of God. We cannot help but be changed. We must be changed (see Titus 1:1).

- How would you describe someone strong in truth and weak in godliness? Or is it even possible to be such?

- How would you describe someone weak in knowledge and strong in godliness? Or is it even possible?

- Which of the two aspects above do you most identify with?

- In what practical ways can we live out knowledge that leads to godliness? How can your group help you in this process?

CHAPTER 3: YOU'LL NEVER RISE ABOVE YOUR LEADER

Biblical Text: Titus 1:5–16

First Reaction

1. What one aspect of this chapter do you hope we as a group would talk about?

Into the Word

1. Who was Titus? Based on the following references (Titus 1:4; Gal. 2:1–3; 2 Cor. 2:13; 8:23), how would you describe him? What was Titus commissioned to do in Crete?

2. Titus 1:5–16 and 1 Timothy 3:1–7 list the qualifications for an elder. Todd organized this list under the two more general qualities of character and conviction.

   - Compare these qualities to a good leader in the secular world. What are the similarities and differences?

   - Based on the emphasis of the text, which qualities are most important?

3. What are the two ministry roles of elders (v. 9)? How can we support them as they carry out these roles?

4. In what way does teaching and holding to sound doctrine encourage, strengthen, and promote a healthier church?

5. In what ways does good leadership beget a zeal for good works?

6. In Hebrews 13:17, we read, "Obey your leaders and submit to them, for they are keeping watch over your souls, as those who will have to give an account. Let them do this with joy and not with groaning, for that would be of no advantage to you." Do you think most Christians consider this a "hard saying"? In light of this verse, what is the responsibility of the leaders, and what is our responsibility?

CHAPTER 4: FIXING THE DISCIPLESHIP DEFICIT

Biblical Text: Titus 2:1–10

First Reaction

1. Consider the people that have discipled you throughout the years, formally or informally. What specifically did they do that stood out to you? Why do these things stand out to you?

Into the Word

1. The phrase "but as for you" indicates that Paul is drawing a contrast to something from prior verses. Reread Titus 1:10–16. How does Paul's exhortation in Titus 2:1 to "teach what accords with sound doctrine" compare to the picture of false teachers in 1:10–16? How does 1:1 negate the idea that the guidelines in the rest of the passage are culturally bound to the first century?

2. Paul presents concrete guidance for character and conduct that corresponds to the Christian faith based on age and gender. List the guidelines for each group. Compare the similarities and distinctives for each group. Why do you suspect Paul gets specific (speaking to people of different genders and ages) when discussing behavioral expectations of the church?

Older Men	*Older Women*
Young Men	*Young Women*
Slaves	

3. Paul mentions some items that he hopes result from biblical teaching. What are they (see Titus 2:5, 8, 10)? In what ways are these consequences similar to the qualifications for elders in Titus 1?

4. Modeling and mentoring are major themes in this passage and are activities that the entire congregation should be engaged in. Can you share any examples of modeling or mentoring from your own life? What are the obstacles that cause us to leave the teaching to others in the church? What are some concrete ways you can intentionally model and mentor others?

5. The essence of Todd's point in this chapter was that biblical teaching catalyzes and concretizes zeal for good works. Can you think of specific instances when the teaching ministry at your church has resulted in this happening?

6. Learning sound doctrine does not automatically result in living a life of good works. What are some things we can do to bridge the gap between being taught sound doctrine and living a life of good works? How do preaching, church leadership, and teaching help address this issue?

CHAPTER 5: WHAT GOD DOES MATTERS MORE

Biblical Text: Titus 2:11–15

First Reaction

1. What one aspect of this chapter do you hope we as a group would talk about?

Into the Word

1. What new insights or perspective did you gain on the concept of grace?

2. One of the characteristics of grace is that it is possessive. How does this truth promote our being zealous for good works?

3. Paul identifies two critical steps we need to take in order to be trained by grace. Why are these two steps so effective in training us? How can you better take these steps in your own life?

4. Consider times when you have been waiting. Would you define these instances as passive or active waiting? Provide examples of active waiting. What can we do to make our waiting active?

CHAPTER 6: STOP, LOOK, AND LISTEN

Biblical Text: Titus 3:1–7

First Reaction

1. If you were to summarize the main point of this chapter in your own words, what would you say it is?

Into the Word

1. In light of Titus 3:2, what does it look like to be a quarrelsome Christian? How do we balance upholding truth and our social responsibility?

2. In Titus 3:3, Paul lists ways "we . . . were once." Can you identify with any of these that he lists (for example, "foolish, disobedient, led astray, slaves to various passions and pleasures, passing our days in malice and envy, hated by others and hating one another")?

   - How might your past life lead to an attitude of disdain?

   - Are there any disdainful attitudes that you are prone to?

   - Explain how the gospel addresses our attitudes of disdain and arrogance.

3. To help us better recognize the needs around us, Todd suggested (per Tim Keller) that we should stop, look, and listen. If you have taken time to stop, look, and listen, what specific needs have you observed? What steps have you taken to meet those needs?

4. As a group, discuss what the practical, tangible needs in your community are, and what your group can do collectively to stop, look, and listen in order to begin meeting those needs.

CHAPTER 7: GIVE CHIEF ATTENTION TO THE CHIEF THINGS

Biblical Text: Titus 3:8–11

First Reaction

1. What one aspect of this chapter do you hope we as a group would talk about?

2. Have you ever found yourself caught up in "mouse-hunting"? If so, what was the experience? How did you recognize that your priorities were misaligned?

Into the Word

1. Based on Titus 3:8, why is it easy to lose our focus on the gospel truth?

2. What does it look like to "hammer on the gospel" in your personal life? How can hammering on the gospel apply to your small group?

3. How does lack of focus on the gospel keep us from being zealous for good works?

4. Titus 3:9 instructs us to avoid foolish controversies. Todd shared three patterns of behavior common in foolish controversies. They are:

   A. Quarreling over minor doctrinal points as though they were major truths of the faith (making a mountain out of a molehill).

B. Engaging in debate or disputes in the wrong way or with the wrong methods.

C. Debating for the wrong reasons or with the wrong goals in mind.

Is there a behavior (A, B, or C) that you are prone to? If so, which one?

5. If common foolish controversies in the first century included genealogies, dissensions, and quarrels about the Law, what are some modern-day foolish controversies?

6. What are some loving ways we can steer away from and diffuse foolish controversies?

7. If focusing on the gospel helps us devote ourselves to good works, how then does focusing on foolish controversies or not addressing a divisive individual detract from a life of good works?

CHAPTER 8: DEVOTED TO GOOD WORKS

Biblical Text: Titus 3:12–15

First Reaction

1. What one aspect of this chapter do you hope we as a group would talk about?

Into the Word

1. Considering the definition of good works from Titus 3:12–14, why do you think all three elements (human acts, meeting gospel needs, done in Jesus' name) are necessary?

2. Since learning comes by doing, what are some ways we can do good works?

3. What are urgent gospel needs you see? As individuals? As a group?

4. What is your reaction to John Stott's vision of a serving church?

Acknowledgments

I am grateful to Moody Publishers for their support of this project and their excellent stewardship of the manuscript. Special thanks to Drew Dyck and Kevin Emmert for their expertise and encouragement along the way. This book began its life as a sermon series preached at Calvary Memorial Church in Oak Park, Illinois. From 2008 to 2018, I had the privilege of serving as the Senior Pastor of the church. Those were rich and rewarding years, a wonderful decade of what Dietrich Bonhoeffer would call "life together."

Notes

Introduction: Ancient Wisdom for Today's Church

1. Will Mancini, *Church Unique: How Missional Leaders Cast Vision, Capture Culture, and Create Movement* (San Francisco: Jossey-Bass, 2008). See chapter 1, "Unoriginal Sin: Neglecting Uniqueness," pages 5–16.
2. Dallas Willard, "Discipleship: For Super-Christians Only?" in *Christianity Today* (October 10, 1980), now reprinted in Dallas Willard, *The Spirit of the Disciplines: Understanding How God Changes Lives* (San Francisco: Harper-Collins, 1988), 258–65, citations found on 258 and 259 (respectively).
3. Ibid., 259 (emphasis original).
4. Gabe Lyons and David Kinnaman, *unChristian: What a New Generation Really Things about Christianity* (Grand Rapids: Baker Books, 2007), 42.
5. See Gordon D. Fee, *1 and 2 Timothy, Titus*, New International Biblical Commentary, vol. 13 (Peabody, MA: Hendrickson, 1988), 11–12.

Chapter 1: Why Titus?

1. Among commentators, Gordon D. Fee, *1 and 2 Timothy, Titus*, New International Biblical Commentary, vol. 13 (Peabody, MA: Hendrickson, 1988), 11–12, in particular has stressed this point.

Chapter 2: What Turns a Place Upside Down?

1. C. H. Spurgeon, *The Early Years 1834–1859* (London: Banner of Truth, 1962), 193.
2. Ibid.
3. D. Martyn Lloyd-Jones, *Preaching and Preachers* (Grand Rapids: Zondervan, 1972), 297.
4. John Stott, *The Living Church* (Downers Grove, IL: InterVarsity Press, 2007), 97.
5. See D. Martyn Lloyd-Jones, *Preaching and Preachers* (Grand Rapids: Zondervan, 2011), 17–32.

6. John A. Broadus, *On the Preparation and Delivery of Sermons*, 4th ed., revised by Vernon L. Stanfield (San Francisco: HarperCollins, 1979), 3, cited in Albert R. Mohler, *He Is Not Silent: Preaching in a Postmodern World* (Chicago: Moody Publishers, 2008), 16.

7. Quoted in Mohler, *He Is Not Silent*, 47.

8. The "and" (*kai*) is epexegetic, further explaining what is entailed in faith. See I. H. Marshall, *The Pastoral Epistles*, ICC (London: T & T Clark, 1999), 121.

9. I owe this observation to Lloyd-Jones, *Preaching and Preachers*, 28.

10. Matthew Parris, "As an atheist, I truly believe Africa needs God," *The Times*, December 27, 2008.

Chapter 3: You'll Never Rise Above Your Leader

1. Alexander Strauch, *Biblical Eldership* (Littleton: Lewis and Roth, 1995), 15.

2. See I. H. Marshall, *The Pastoral Epistles*, ICC (London: T & T Clark, 1999), 155–57, who provides a succinct assessment of the five main interpretations. Part of the difficulty with the expression is that it is found only in the New Testament and not in any extrabiblical sources contemporaneous with the New Testament.

3. Gordon D. Fee, *1 and 2 Timothy, Titus*, New International Biblical Commentary, Vol. 13 (Peabody, MA: Hendrickson, 1988), 173.

4. Cited in John R. W. Stott, *Guard the Truth: The Message of 1 Timothy and Titus*, Bible Speaks Today (Downers Grove, IL: InterVarsity Press, 1996), 179.

5. See Alexander Strauch, *Biblical Eldership: An Urgent Call to Restore Biblical Church Leadership* (Colorado Springs: Lewis & Roth, 2003), 15–34, on pastoral leadership, where he identifies the four critical functions of biblical eldership mentioned here and elaborates on them each in turn.

Chapter 4: Fixing the Discipleship Deficit

1. Dallas Willard, "Discipleship: For Super-Christians Only?" in *Christianity Today* (October 10, 1980), now reprinted in Dallas Willard, *The Spirit of the Disciplines: Understanding How God Changes Lives* (San Francisco: Harper-Collins, 1988), 258.

2. Ibid., 259.

3. Ajith Fernando, *The Call to Joy and Pain: Embracing Suffering in Your Ministry* (Wheaton: Crossway, 2007), 157–58.

4. Andrew Murray, *How to Raise Your Children for Christ* (Minneapolis: Bethany House, 1975), 12.

5. The quote from Chesterton is, "The Christian ideal has not been tried and found wanting. It has been found difficult; and left untried." G. K. Chesterton, "The Unfinished Temple," in *What's Wrong with the World*, in *The Collected Works of G. K. Chesterton*, vol. 4 (San Francisco: Ignatius Press, 1987), 61.

Chapter 5: What God Does Matters More

1. John Calvin, *Institutes of the Christian Religion*, trans. for Lewis Battles, ed. John T. McNeill (Philadelphia: Westminster, 1970), 3.7.3. Calvin understood self-denial to be the sum of the Christian life.

Chapter 6: Stop, Look, and Listen

1. Cited in Rodney Stark, *The Rise of Christianity: How the Obscure, Marginal Jesus Movement Became the Dominant Religious Force in the Western World in a Few Centuries* (San Francisco: Harper Collins, 1997), 82.

2. John Calvin, *Institutes of the Christian Religion*, trans. for Lewis Battles, ed. John T. McNeill (Philadelphia: Westminster, 1970), 3.7.4.

3. Here I am indebted to John Stott's fine exposition of these verses. See John R. W. Stott, *Guard the Truth: The Message of 1 Timothy and Titus*, Bible Speaks Today (Downers Grove, IL: InterVarsity Press, 1996), 202–206.

4. Timothy J. Keller, *Ministries of Mercy: The Call of the Jericho Road*, second edition (Phillipsburg, NJ: P&R Publishing, 1997), 127.

5. Ibid.

Chapter 7: Give Chief Attention to the Chief Things

1. This and other citations taken from C. H. Spurgeon, *The Complete John Ploughman*, C. H. Spurgeon Classics (Fearn, Ross-shire, Scotland: Christian Focus Publications, 2007), 214–16.

2. C. H. Spurgeon, *Lectures to My Students* (Grand Rapids: Zondervan, 1979), 78.

3. Ibid.

4. C. H. Spurgeon, *The Complete John Ploughman: John Ploughman's Talk and John Ploughman's Pictures* (Ross-Shire, Scotland: Christian Focus, 2007), 216.

Chapter 8: Devoted to Good Works

1. Richard Sterns, *The Hole in Our Gospel: What Does God Expect of Us? The Answer That Changed My Life and Might Just Change the World* (Nashville: Thomas Nelson, 2014), xxv.

2. Ibid., xxvi.

3. I. H. Marshall, *The Pastoral Epistles*, ICC (London: T & T Clark, 1999), 345.

4. Jerome D. Quinn, *The Letter to Titus*, Anchor 35 (New Haven, CT: Yale University Press, 2005), 267: "The learning urged here is no abstract, theological systematization. It is learning charity by acting charitably."

5. William D. Mounce, *Pastoral Epistles*, Word Biblical Commentary, vol. 46 (Waco, TX: Thomas Nelson, 2000), 457.

6. Quinn, *The Letter to Titus*, 267.

7. John R. W. Stott, *The Living Church: Convictions of a Lifelong Pastor* (Downers Grove, IL: InterVarsity Press, 2007), 168–69.

Epilogue: A City on a Hill

1. See Jonathan Edwards, "A City on a Hill," in *Sermons and Discourses 1734–1738* in *The Works of Jonathan Edwards,* vol. 19 (New Haven: Yale, 2001), 537–59.

2. Ibid., 543.

3. Ibid., 544.

WHAT DOES THE CHURCH NEED TO HEAR TODAY?

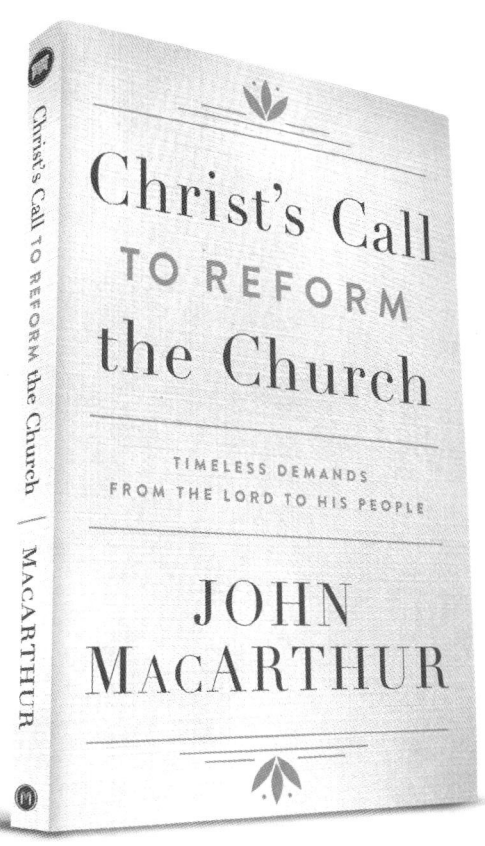

WHO IS THE HOLY SPIRIT ANYWAY?

DIG DEEP INTO THE WHOLE NEW TESTAMENT!

MACARTHUR NEW TESTAMENT COMMENTARY SERIES

The set includes:

Matthew (4 volumes)	Galatians	Hebrews
Mark (2 volumes)	Ephesians	James
Luke (4 volumes)	Philippians	1 Peter
John (2 volumes)	Colossians & Philemon	2 Peter and Jude
Acts (2 volumes)	1 & 2 Thessalonians	1–3 John
Romans (2 volumes)	1 Timothy	Revelation (2 volumes)
1 Corinthians	2 Timothy	Index
2 Corinthians	Titus	

MOODY
Publishers®

From the Word to Life®

This bestselling 34-volume hardcover commentary set features verse-by-verse interpretation and rich application of God's Word. Easy to understand, yet rich in scholarly background.

978-0-8024-1347-5 | also available as an eBook

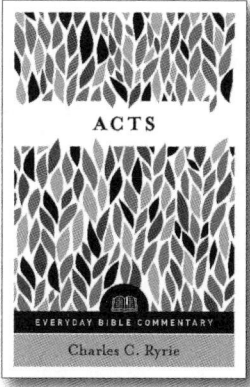
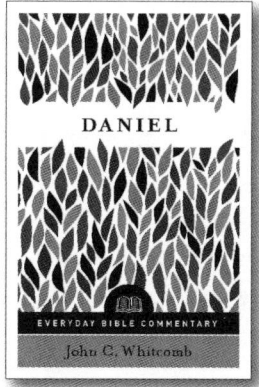
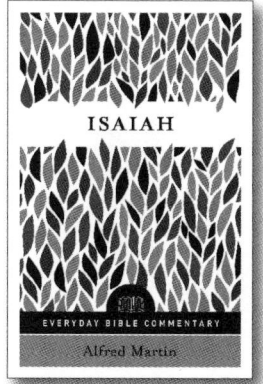

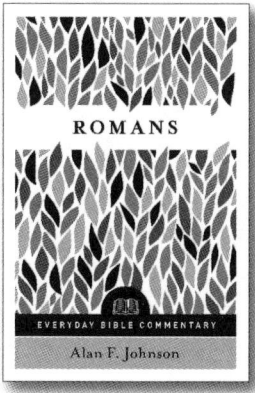